Epochs of Ancient History

EDITED BY

REV. G. W. COX, M.A. AND CHARLES SANKEY, M. A.

ROMAN HISTORY—The EARLY EMPIRE

W. W. CAPES, M.A.

ROMAN HISTORY

THE EARLY EMPIRE

FROM THE ASSASSINATION OF JULIUS CÆSAR
TO THAT OF DOMITIAN

BY

W. W. CAPES, M.A.

LATE FELLOW AND TUTOR OF QUEEN'S COLLEGE, AND
READER IN ANCIENT HISTORY IN THE UNIVERSITY OF OXFORD

WITH TWO MAPS

NEW YORK
SCRIBNER, ARMSTRONG & CO.

GRANT, FAIRES & RODGERS,
Electrotypers & Printers,
52 & 54 North Sixth Street, Philadelphia.

CONTENTS.

INTRODUCTORY CHAPTER.

CHAPTER I.

AUGUSTUS B. C. 31—A. D. 14.

CHAPTER II.

TIBERIUS: A.D. 14–37.

CHAPTER III.

CALIGULA: A.D. 37-41.

CHAPTER IV.

CLAUDIUS: A.D. 41-54.

CHAPTER V.

NERO: A.D. 54–68.

CHAPTER VI.

GALBA: A.D. 68–69.

CHAPTER VII.

OTHO: A.D. 69.

CHAPTER VIII.

VITELLIUS: A.D. 69.

CHAPTER IX.

VESPASIAN; A.D. 69–79.

CHAPTER X.

TITUS: A.D. 79–81.

CHAPTER XI.

DOMITIAN: A.D. 81–96.

CHAPTER XII.

THE POSITION OF THE EMPEROR.

CHAPTER XIII.

THE RIGHTS OF ROMAN CITIZENSHIP.

CHAPTER XIV.

LIFE IN THE PROVINCES.

CHAPTER XV.

THE STATE OF TRADE.

CHAPTER XVI.

THE GROWING DEPOPULATION OF ITALY AND GREECE.

CHAPTER XVII.

THE FRONTIERS AND THE ARMY.

CHAPTER XVIII.

THE MORAL STANDARD OF THE AGE.

CHAPTER XIX.

THE REVIVAL OF RELIGIOUS SENTIMENT.

The Chief Original Authorities for the History of the First Century.

Appian, "Civil Wars": for the period of the civil struggle.

Dion Cassius, "Roman History."

Inscriptionum Latinarum Corpus: Auctoritate Acad. Berol. ed.

Josephus: for the Jewish war.

"Monumentum Ancyranum v. Res. gestæ divi Augusti": ed. Th. Mommsen.

Pliny, "Letters": for the close of the period.

Plutarch, "Lives of Julius Cæsar, Cicero, Antonius, M. Brutus Galba, Otho."

Seneca, in the historical illustrations of his moral treatises.

Suetonius, "Lives of the Cæsars."

Tacitus, "Annals and Histories."

Velleius Paterculus, for the reigns of Augustus and Tiberius.

Of the poets: Horace, Juvenal, and Martial especially illustrate the history of the period.

MAPS.

18

Genealogical Tables.

I.

Caius Julius Cæsar=Aurelia.

C. JULIUS CÆSAR Dictator=Cornelia.

Julia=Cn. Pompeius Magnus.

Julia=M. Attius Balbus.

Attia=C. Octavius.

(1) Claudia
(2) Scribonia = C. Octavius afterwards C. Julius Cæsar Octavianus AUGUSTUS.=(3) Livia Drusilla.

(2) M. Agrippa=Julia={(1) M. Marcellus.
(3) TIBERIUS Nero Emp.

C. Cæsar. L. Cæsar. Agrippina=Germanicus. (v. Table II.) Julia Minor. Agrippa Postumus.

(2) M. Antonius triumvir=Octavia=(1) M. Claudius Marcellus.

M. Claudius Marcellus=Julia d. of Augustus

L. Domitius Ahenobarbus=Antonia Major.

Antonia Minor =Nero Claudius Drusus (v. Table II.)

Cn. Domitius Ahenobarbus =Agrippina Minor.

Domitia Lepida=M. Valerius Messalinus.

L. Domitius Ahenobarbus (NERO).

Messalina, Wife of Claudius.

Genealogical Tables (continued)

II.

Tib. Claudius Nero=Livia Drusilla.

T. Pomponius Atticus.

M. Vipsanius Agrippa=Pomponia.

Nero Claudius Drusus=Antonia Minor.
(v. Table I.)

Tiberius Claudius Nero=Vipsania Agrippina.

Germanicus=Agrippina Major.

Ti. Claudius Nero=(1) Messalina.
(2) Agrippina Minor.

Livilla=Nero Claudius Drusus Cæsar.

Nero Cæsar.

Drusus Cæsar.

C. Cæsar Caligula =Cæsonia.

Agrippina Minor=(1) Cn. Domitius Ahenobarbus.
(2) Crispus Passienus.
(3) Ti. Claudius Emp.

Julia=Nero Cæsar, Son of Germanicus.

Tiberius, Gemellus.

Julia. Drusilla.

L. Domitius Ahenobarbus Nero = Octavia

Britannicus.

III.

? Manceps Operarum (Suet. 1).

T. Flavius Petro.

Vespasius Pollio.

Vespasia Polla=(T. Flavius) Sabinus.

Flavius Sabinus.

T. Flavius Vespasianus=Domitilla.

Cn. Domitius Corbulo.

Titus Flav. Vesp.=Marcia.

Domitilla

Domitianus=Domitia Longina.

Julia.

ROMAN HISTORY.

THE EARLIER EMPIRE.

INTRODUCTION.

Rapid survey of the history of Rome from the death of Julius Cæsar to the battle of Actium.

THE genius and statesmanship of Julius Cæsar secured only a few years of absolute power, and had not time enough to shape the forms of empire, or carry out far-reaching plans. When he fell under the daggers of his murderers, he left no system of established rule, and no successor to replace him. The Commonwealth had been discredited by years of impotence; anarchy at home, misgovernment abroad had shown the breakdown of the ancient institutions of the state, and the frail plant of liberty needed more to bring it back to healthy life than to be watered with the blood of Cæsar. But when the young Octavius left his books at Apollonia, and came to Rome to claim his rights, few could have had serious fears of his ambition, or could have foreseen in him the man who was to close the drama of the great Republic and bring the empire on the stage. For he had played no part as yet in public life, was known to be of feeble health, had given no proof of genius or of self-reliant courage. Sent on before to the advanced camp in Epirus, to be ready for campaigns in the far East, he was startled from his round of rhetoric and drill by the news of his great uncle's murder. He crossed the sea without delay; and hearing on his way B.C. 44. that his kinsman's will had named him heir, he took at once the name of Cæsar Octavianus, and hurried on to claim his heritage at Rome. His mother told him of her fear, his stepfather urged the need of caution, and pointed to the dangers in his way; but he persisted, though almost alone, and though he saw the need to be resolute and wary. The daggers that had been sharpened against Julius might be drawn upon himself, if he spoke too openly of vengeance, or appealed at once to the soldiers and the people. The name that he had just assumed had an ominous sound in the ears of Senate and of nobles; and M. Antonius, the old confidant and partisan of Cæsar, by right of his authority as consul, had taken the reins of power into his hands, had gained possession of the treasures and the papers of the fallen ruler, and was in no mood to share them with a rival claimant. The conduct of Octavianus, though bold, was very politic and far-sighted. Resolved at any cost to show respect for the last wishes of his kinsman, he drew largely on the means of his family or friends to pay the legacies bequeathed by Cæsar to every citizen of Rome, and defrayed even the expenses of the public shows that had been promised. He paid his court with tact to the members of the Senate, and talked of amnesty and peace; put on a show of winning deference for the leaders of the moderate party, and for Cicero above all, and fed their hopes, that they might find in his growing popularity a harmless counterpoise to the violent ambition of Antonius. Even when forced at last to arm in self-defence, and to levy troops among the veterans of

Cæsar, he courted the old statesman still; he played upon his vanity, and called him father. Affecting to draw his sword only in defence of the constitution and the Senate, he offered to serve with his own legions under the new consuls against Antonius, the common enemy of all loyal citizens. But he clearly read the jealous suspicions of the nobles, and had no mind to be used awhile and then thrown aside like a dishonored tool. So, after the successes won at Mutina, B.C. 43. which cost the lives of both the consuls, he flung away the mask that he had worn, came to terms of union with Antonius and with Lepidus, the governor of Gaul, and marched with his soldiers straight to Rome to wrest the consulship from the reluctant Senate. Then the era of Proscriptions opened, for the confederates agreed to cement their league with blood. Each marked his victims' names upon the fatal list, and each consented to give up adherents of his own to the greed or hatred of his colleagues. Meanwhile the Senatorian party, crushed at Rome, was gathering fresh strength beyond the seas. Brutus in Macedonia, Cassius in Syria, the foremost of the murderers of Cæsar, had turned the provinces which they governed into one vast recruiting-ground for a last decisive struggle. When all was ready they combined their forces and offered battle to the enemies who had crossed over to attack them. Once more came the crash of mighty armies met again B.C. 42. in civil war, and the battle-fields of Philippi saw the fall of the last of the great republicans of Rome.

The world lay prostrate at the conquerors' feet; it remained only to divide the spoil. Antonius stayed behind to organize and rule the East. The Province of Africa was thought enough to content the absent Lepidus, while Italy and all the West fell to the portion of Octavianus.

But still as the young schemer mounted higher the dangers seemed to thicken in his path, to test his hardihood and patient statecraft. He returned to Italy to find an exhausted treasury and half-ruined people; veterans clamoring for their pay and settling with fierce eagerness upon the promised lands; peasants ousted from their homes, taken to brigandage from sheer despair; the city populace in no loyal mood to a master who had little to bestow; while the wife and brother of his rival fanned the smouldering discontent, and vexed him sorely with intrigues, then flew to arms at last, and when beaten stood sullenly at bay within the beleagured fortress of Perusia. The sea meanwhile was at the mercy of the bold Sextus Pompeius, who scoured the coasts of Italy with galleys manned by motley crews of republicans who had fought under his father's lead, of pirates to whom that father's name had been once a sound of terror, of ruined victims of the late proscriptions, of slaves and runaways of every class. The corn-ships dared not venture near the blockaded ports, and prices mounted to famine height, till the starving population rose in fierce mutiny against their ruler; while Antonius was on his way with a great fleet to call him to account for the treatment of his brother, who had hardly escaped with life from the horrors of the siege. But Italy was sick of civil war. The soldiers, tired of constant bloodshed, made their leaders sheath their swords and join in league and amity, in pledge of which Antonius took to wife Octavia, the sister of his rival, while Sextus bargained as the price of peace to keep his hold upon the islands and the sea, and Lepidus, displaced already from his office of command, held only in his feeble grasp the dignity and functions of High Pontiff.

B. C. 41.

For six more years of divided power Octavianus schemed, and toiled, and waited. He secured his hold on Italy, calmed the elements of disorder in its midst, refilled the treasury and stocked the granaries, till he felt himself strong enough to defy Sextus on the seas and crush the bold buccaneer after many a hard-fought struggle. At last, but not till all was safe elsewhere, came the crisis of the duel with Antonius. Eastern luxury had done its work upon his passionate nature. Slothful self-indulgence, broken only by fitful moods of fiery energy, clouded his reason and unnerved his manhood. The Egyptian Cleopatra had lured him with her blandishments and wound her snares around his heart, till Rome heard with indignation of the wrongs of the forsaken wife and of the orgies of the wanton pair. Nay, more, they heard that not content with parodying the names and attributes of foreign gods, they claimed the right to change the seat of empire and make Alexandria the new capital of the Roman world. Was the dignity of a chaste matron, it was asked, to be the sport of the minions of an Eastern court? Should Octavianus tamely wait to see the national honor further outraged, and the monstrous forms of uncouth worships install themselves, within the Seven Hills and drive the old deities from their venerable shrines? The personal quarrel was transformed into a war of creeds and races. In place of the horrors of a civil struggle men thought only of the motley aggregate of foreign peoples arrayed at Actium in the extravagance of barbaric pomp against the discipline and valor of the West.

In the actual conflict Antonius displayed neither a general's skill nor a soldier's courage. He fought, seemingly, to cover a retreat that had been planned before. Cleopatra's galleys gave the B. C. 31.

signal for the flight, and the leader of what was now a hopeless cause hastened after her to Egypt, where he found discontent and treachery spread around him. After a few months spent in moody despair or riotous excesses he died by his own hand, to be soon followed by his paramour to his dishonored grave.

CHAPTER I.

AUGUSTUS: B.C. 31—A.D. 14.

The remarkable change in Octavianus after he gained absolute power

THE victory of Actium had made Octavianus the undisputed master of the Roman world. One by one rivals and obstacles had been swept away, and the patient schemer had now mounted to the topmost round of the ladder of ambition. During the troublous years of the long struggle for power his public life had been one course of selfish aims, unscrupulous acts, and makeshift policy; he had yet to prove that there was anything of real and abiding greatness in his schemes to raise him from the ranks of mere political adventurers. But from this time we may trace a seeming change of character, which is the more remarkable because it is so hard to parallel.

not a mere change of policy,

It was no change of measures only, such as often comes with new conditions, such as that which made the founder of the dynasty reverse much of the policy of earlier years.

For, spendthrift and prodigal as Julius had been before, he used his power to curtail extravagance, sent police agents to the markets, and even to the houses of the wealthy, to put down luxury by force; the leader of the popular party forbade the growth of guilds and social clubs like those which had often carried the elections in his favor; the favorite of the populace was anxious to check the pride of pauperism by sterner measures; the revolutionary general whose tent had been the refuge of the men of tarnished name and ruined fortunes baffled all their hopes of plunder, by passing stringent measures to restore credit and to curb official greed. Octavianus also in like case resorted to like policy. One of his first cares was to repeal the unconstitutional acts of his earlier life, and so to close the period of revolution. He took steps without delay to restore order and to strengthen the moral safeguards which years of anarchy and civil war had almost ruined. To this end he passed laws like those of Julius, and, unlike his kinsman, was enabled by his long tenure of power to carry out a conservative reform in morals and religion which left some enduring traces.

But the change in character lay deeper far than this. He had shown while the struggle lasted a cruelty without excuse. Though possibly reluctant at the first to engage in the proscriptions, he is said to have acted in them more relentlessly than either of his colleagues; he had his prisoners of war butchered in cold blood, mocked at their prayers for decent burial, and calmly watched their dying agonies.

but of temper and demeanor.

That he was hard and pitiless beyond the spirit of his times is implied in many stories of the day, and among others we read that when the captives of Philippi passed in bonds before their conquerors they saluted Antonius with marked respect, but vented their deepest curses on Octavianus to his face.

But after Actium he showed what was for that age an unusual clemency. He spared his open enemies, he hunted out no victims, and professed even to burn the secret papers of his rival which might have compromised his partisans at Rome. The same gentler spirit breathes through the whole of his long period of rule. His jealous intolerance had led him once to drive a consul elect to suicide for a bitter word, and to fine or banish citizens of Nursia for honoring with a monument their dead who had fallen, as they wrote, in defence of freedom on the field of Mutina. But he was ready now to show respect to the memory of Pompeius, to let historians write the praises of the great republicans of Rome, to congratulate the men of Mediolanum (Milan) for prizing the busts of Brutus, to listen calmly to the gibes vented on himself in popular satires or in dead men's wills, to let even lampoons be scattered in the Senate House, and make no effort to hunt out the authors. His suspicious fears had made him once give orders for the instant execution of a curious bystander who had pressed in too eagerly to hear him speak in public, and put even to the torture a prætor who came to greet him, and whose hidden note book was mistaken for a dagger; but in later life he walked without an escort through the streets, went to and fro to join the social gatherings of his friends, and showed no fear of an assassin's knife. The cheerful cordiality and homely courtesies of his maturer age were a marked contrast to the cold, ungenial reserve of earlier days; and those who find his real character hard to read may see perhaps a fitting symbol of it in the figure of the Sphinx which he wore upon his signet-ring.

The change was too great to be easily made.

But this change of manner could not be an easy thing, and was probably not soon effected. There are signs which seem to show that constant watchfulness and self-restraint were needed to curb his natural temper, and that personal influences were at work to help him. Though he was patient and merciful in most cases that were brought before him when on the seat of judgment, it is said that Mæcenas, who was standing by, marked on one occasion the old blood-thirsty instinct reappear, and flung to him a hasty note with the words "Rise, Hangman!" written on it. Another time, when stung by what was uttered in the Senate, he hurried out abruptly, and excused himself afterwards for want of courtesy by saying that he feared his anger would slip from his control. We are told that with others commonly, and even with Livia, his wife, he would not always trust himself to speak on subjects of grave moment without writing down the notes of what he had to say. In the gloom that settled on him in old age, when family losses and dishonor, coupled with national disasters, weighed upon his mind, the hard, unlovely features of his character, long hidden out of sight, seemed to come to light once more as the force of self-control was weakened by the laws of natural decay. Yet even with such reserves his history presents a spectacle almost unexampled of the force of will in moulding and tempering an ungenial nature, and of the chastening influence of sovereign rule. The signal victory just won, the honors voted by the servile Senate, the acclamations of the people, the license of unbounded power, might well have turned his head, as they proved fatal to the temper of many a later emperor; but the dagger of Brutus haunted his memory and warned him to beware of outraging Roman feeling.

Called for watchfulness and self-restraint.

But, far beyond its effect upon his personal bearing, we may trace the influence of these warning memories on the work which lay before him, of giving shape and system to the future government

The change in the forms of the Constitution.

of Rome. Power and repute had passed away from the old forms of the Republic. The whole world lay at the feet of the master of many legions; it remained only to define the constitutional forms in which the new forces were to work. But to do this was no easy task. The perplexities of his position, the fears and hopes that crossed his mind, are thrown into dramatic form by the historian Dion Cassius, who brings a scene before our fancy in which Octavianus listens to the conflicting counsels of his two great advisers Agrippa and Mæcenas. The former is supposed to paint in sombre colors the difficulties of a monarch's lot, to remind him of the warnings of the past and the dangers of the future, and strongly to urge him to copy the example set by Sulla, and after passing needful laws, and strengthening the safeguards against anarchy and license, to resign the outward show of power and come down from the dizzy pinnacle of greatness. Mæcenas, on the other hand, counsels absolute rule, though masked by constitutional disguises and describes at great length a system of centralized government, in sketching which the historian drew mainly from the experience of his own later times, and with slight regard for historic truth, attributed to the inventive genius of Mæcenas a full-grown system of political machinery which took some centuries of imperialism to develop. But though we must regard the narrative in question more as the writer's own political theorizing than as a sketch of matter of fact, yet there is little doubt that the schemes of resignation were at some time discussed by the Emperor and by his circle of advisers. It is even possible, as the same writer tells us, that he laid before the Senators at this time some proposal to leave the helm of state and

The debate on the subject in Dion Cassius.

The proposal to resign.

let them guide it as of old. We are told that they were thrown into confusion by his words, and that, mistrusting his sincerity, or fearing the return of anarchy and the scramble for power that would soon ensue, they all implored him to withdraw his words and take back the power which he had resigned. The scene, if ever really acted, was but an idle comedy, and the offer could scarcely have been seriously meant, though there may have been some passing thought of it even at this time and still more at a later period, when he had long been sated with power and burdened with the cares of office. It is more probable that he was content with some faint show of resistance, when the Senate heaped their honors on his head, as afterwards when, more than once, after a ten years' interval they solemnly renewed the tenure of his power.

Sincerely wishes to avoid the title of King,

But we cannot doubt his sincerity in one respect—in his wish to avoid the kingly title and all the odious associations of the name. It had been from early times offensive to Roman ears; it had grown far more so as they heard more of the wanton lust and cruelty and haughtiness of Eastern monarchs, and they scorned to be degraded themselves to the level of their cringing subjects. The charge of aspiring to be king had often been an ominous cry in party struggles, and had proved fatal to more than one great leader; it had been truly said perhaps of Cæsar, and had largely helped to ruin him, and his successor was too wary to be dazzled by the bauble of a name. He shrank also from another title, truly Roman in its character, but odious since the days of Sulla; and though the populace of Rome, when panic-struck by pestilence and famine, clamored to have him made dictator, and threatened to

or of Dictator.

burn the Senate as it sat in council if their will was not obeyed, yet nothing would induce him to bear the hateful name. But the name of Cæsar he had taken long ago, after his illustrious uncle's death, and this became the title first of the dynasty and then of the imperial office. Besides this he allowed himself to be styled Augustus, a name which roused no jealousy and outraged no Roman sentiment, yet vaguely implied some dignity and reverence from its long association with the objects of religion. As such he preferred it to the suggested name of Romulus, and allowed one of the months to be so called after him, as the preceding one of Julius had been named after his kinsman. With this exception he assumed no new symbol of monarchic power, but was satisfied with the old official titles, which though charged with memories of the Republic, yet singly corresponded to some side or fragment of absolute authority. The first of these was Imperator, which served to connect him with the army. The *imperium* which the name expressed, has stood in earlier days for the higher functions, more especially for the power of the sword, which belonged to civil as well as military authority. But, gradually curtailed in other cases by the jealousy of the republic, it had kept its full meaning only in the camp; the imperator was the general in command, or, in a still more special case, he was the victorious leader whose soldiers had saluted him upon the field of battle. Julius, whose veterans had often greeted him with this title in many a hard-fought campaign, chose it seemingly as a fitting symbol of the new *régime*, as a frank avowal of its military basis, and in this sense it was found convenient by his successors. It implied absolute

Had already taken the name of Cæsar.

Is styled. Augustus.

Takes the old republican titles.

Imperator.

authority, such as the general has over his soldiers, and the concentration in a single chief of the wide-spread powers entrusted to subordinate commanders; it suggested little of the old forms of constitutional election, but appealed rather to the memory of the army's loyal acclamations, and gave seeming claim to their entire obedience.

The title of the tribunician power connected the monarch with the interest of the lower orders. In the early days of privilege, when Rome was parted into rival classes, the tribunes had been the champions of the commons. Sacrosanct, or inviolate themselves, and armed with power to shield the weak from the license of magistrate or noble, they gradually assumed the right to put a veto or check on all public business in Rome. In the party struggles of the last century of the republic they had abused their constitutional powers to destroy the influence of the Senate and organize the popular movement against the narrow oligarchy of the ruling classes. Such authority was too important to be overlooked or intrusted in its fulness into other hands. The emperor did not, indeed, assume the tribunate, but was vested with the tribunician power which overshadowed the annual holders of the office. It made his person sacred, not in the city only or in discharge of official acts, as in their case, but at all times and through the whole breadth of the empire. It gave him the formal right to call the meetings of the Senate, and to lay before them such business as he pleased, and thus secured the initiative in all concerns of state. Out of the old privilege of appeal to the protection of a tribune came the right of acquittal in judicial functions, which made the Emperor a high court of appeal from all the lower courts, and out of which seem-

Tribunicia Potestas.

ingly has grown the right of pardon vested in the kings of modern Europe. The full meaning and extension of the title seems not to have been discerned at once, but once grasped it was too important to be dropped. By it succeeding emperors dated the tenure of their power, as by the years of a king's reign, and the formal act by which the title was conferred on the kinsman or the confidant who stood nearest to the throne seemed to point him out for succession to the imperial rank.

Princeps.

The familiar name of prince was one of dignity rather than of power. The "princeps senatus" in old days had been the foremost senator of his time, distinguished by weight of character and the experience of high rank, early consulted in debate, and carrying decisive influence by his vote. No one but the Emperor could fill this position safely, and he assumed the name henceforth to connect him with the Senate, as other titles seemed to bind him to the army and the people.

Pontifex Maximus.

For the post of Supreme Pontiff, Augustus was content to wait awhile, until it passed by death from the feeble hands of Lepidus. He then claimed the exclusive tenure of the office, and after this time Pontifex Maximus was always added to the long list of imperial titles. It put into his hands, as the highest functionary of religion, the control of all the ritual of the State; it was a convenient instrument for his policy of conservative reform, and associated with his name some of the reverence that gathered round the domain of spiritual life. Besides these titles to which he assumed an exclusive right he also filled occasionally and for short periods most of the republican offices of higher rank, both in the capital and in the country towns. He took from time to time the consular power, with its august traditions and imposing ceremonial. The authority of censor lay ready to his hands when a moral reform was to be set on foot, and a return attempted to the severity of ancient manners, or when the Senate was to be purged of unworthy members and the order of the *equites* or knights to be reviewed and its dignity consulted. Beyond the capital the proconsular power was vested in him without local limitations, and gave him the right to issue his instructions to the commanders of the legions, as the great generals of the republic had done before. Finally he deigned often to accept offices of local dignity in the smaller towns throughout the empire, appointing in each case a deputy to discharge the duties of the post.

Potestas Consularis.

Censoria.

Proconsularis.

The offices of the State of Rome, meantime, lasted on from the Republic to the Empire, unchanged in name, and with little seeming change of functions. Consuls, Prætors, Quæstors, Tribunes, and Ædiles rose from the same classes as before, and moved for the most part in the same round of work, though they had lost forever their power of initiative and real control. Elected by the people formerly, but with much sinister influence of bribery and auguries, they were now mainly the nominees of Cæsar, though the forms of popular election were still for a time observed, and though Augustus condescended to canvass in person for his friends and to send letters of commendation for those whom he wished to have elected. The consulship was entirely reserved for his nominees, but passed rapidly from hand to hand, since in order to gratify a larger number it was granted at varying intervals for a few months only. For though it was in fact a political nullity henceforth, and its value lay mainly in the

The old offices of the executive.

evidence of imperial favor or its prospects of provincial office, yet the old dignity lasted still, and for centuries the post was spoken of by Romans as almost the highest prize of their ambition. For lower posts a distinction was observed between the places, generally one-half, reserved entirely for the Emperor to fill with his *candidati Cæsaris*, as they are called in their inscriptions, and those which were left for some show of open voting, though influenced, it might be, by court favor.

The peculiar feature of the old Roman executive had been its want of centralized action. Each magistrate might thwart and check his colleague; the collision between different officials, the power of veto, and the absence of supreme authority might bring the political machinery to a dead lock. The imperial system swept aside these dangers, left each magistrate to the routine of his own work, and made him feel his responsibility to the central chief. It was part of the policy of Augustus to disturb as little as possible the old names and forms of the Republic; to leave their old show and dignity, that those who filled them might seem to be not his own creatures, but the servants of the state. But besides these he set up a number of new offices, often of more real power though of lower rank; he filled the most important of them with his confidants, delegating to them the functions which most needed his control, and in which he could not brook any show of independence, and left behind him the rudiments of a centralized bureaucracy which his successors gradually enlarged. Two terms correspond respectively to two great classes.

New offices created.

The name *præfectus*, the *préfét* of modern France, stood in earlier days for the deputy of any officer of state charged specially to execute some definite work. The præfects of Cæsar were his servants,

Præfectus.

named by him and responsible to him, set to discharge duties which the old constitution had commonly ignored. The prefect of the city had appeared in shadowy form under the Republic to represent the consul in his absence. Augustus felt the need, when called away from Rome, to have some one there whom he could trust to watch the jealous nobles and control the fickle mob. His trustiest confidants, Mæcenas and Agrippa, filled the post, and it became a standing office with a growing sphere of competence, overtopping the magistrates of earlier date.

Præfectus Urbi.

The præfects of the prætorian cohorts first appeared when the Senate formally assigned a body-guard to Augustus later in his reign. The troops were named after the picked soldiers who were quartered round the tents of the generals of the Republic, and when they were concentrated by the city walls their chief commanders soon filled a formidable place in history, and their loyalty or treachery often decided the fate of Rome. Next to these in power and importance came the præfects of the watch—the new police force organized by Augustus as a protection against the dangers of the night; and of the corn supplies of Rome, which were always an object of especial care on the part of the imperial government. And besides these, there were many various duties entrusted by the head of the state to special delegates, both in the capital and through the provinces. The title *procurator*, which has come down to us in the form of "proctor," was at first mainly a term of civil law, and was used for a financial agent or attorney. The officers so called were regarded at first as stewards of the Emperor's property or managers of his private business. They were therefore for some time

Prætoria, vigilum annonæ.

Procuratores.

of humble origin, for the Emperor's household was organized like that of any Roman noble. Slaves or freedmen filled the offices of trust, wrote his letters, kept his books, managed his affairs, and did the work of the treasurers and secretaries of state of later days. Kept within bounds by sterner masters, they abused the confidence of weak emperors, and outraged Roman pride by their wealth, arrogance, and ostentation. The agents of the Emperor's privy purse throughout the provinces were called by the same title, but were commonly of higher rank and more repute.

Such in its bare outline was the executive of the imperial government. We have next to see what was the position of the Senate. That body had been in early times the council summoned to advise the king or consul. By the weight and experience of its members, and their lifelong tenure of office, it soon towered above the short-lived executive, and became the chief moving force at Rome. But the policy of the Gracchi had dealt a fatal blow at its supremacy. Proscriptions and civil wars had thinned its ranks. The first Cæsar had treated it with studied disrespect, and in the subsequent times of anarchy the influence of the order and the reputation of its members had sunk to the lowest depth of degradation. It was one of the first cares of Augustus to restore its credit. At the risk of odium and personal danger he more than once revised the list, and purged it of unworthy members, summoning eminent provincials in their place. He was careful of their outward dignity, and made the capital of a million sesterces a needful condition of the rank. The functions also of the Senate were in theory enlarged. Its decrees on questions brought before it had henceforth the binding force of law. As the popular assemblies ceased to meet for legis-

The Senate.

lation, case after case was submitted to its judgment, till it gained speedily by prescription a jurisdiction of wide range, and before long it decided the elections at its will or registered the nominations of the Emperor.

But the substance of power and independence had passed away from it forever. Matters of great moment were debated first, not in the Senate House, but in a sort of Privy Council formed by the trusted advisers of the Emperor, while the discussions of the larger body served chiefly to mask the forms of absolutism, to feel the pulse of popular sentiment, and to register decisions formed elsewhere. Treated with respect and courtesy by wary princes, the senators were the special mark of the jealousy and greed of the worst rulers.

Privy Council.

If we now turn our thoughts from the centre to the provinces we shall find that the imperial system brought with it more sweeping changes and more real improvement. Almost every country of the Roman world had long been frightfully misgoverned. Towards the end of the Republic there rises from every land a cry in tones that grow ever louder—a cry of misery and despair—that their governors are greedy and corrupt, scandalously indifferent to justice, conniving at the extortion of the Roman capitalists who farmed the tithes and taxes, and of the money-lenders, who had settled like leeches all around them.

The government of the provinces.

The governors who hastened to their provinces after a short tenure of official rank at Rome looked to the emoluments of office to retrieve their fortunes, exhausted frequently by public shows and bribery at home. They abused their power in a hundred ways to amass enormous wealth, with little check from the public opinion of their order, or from the courts of law before which they might possibly be prosecuted by their victims or their rivals.

Senatorial provinces.

But a new order of things was now begun. Augustus left to the Senate the nominal control of the more peaceful provinces, which needed little military force. To these ex-consuls and ex-prætors were sent out as before, but with no power of the sword and little of the purse. High salaries were paid to them directly by the state, but the sources of indirect gains were gradually cut off. By their side was a proctor of the Emperor's privy purse, to watch their conduct and report their misdemeanors. At home there was a vigilant ruler, ready to give ear to the complaints of the provincials, and to see that justice was promptly done by the tribunals or the Senate. Doubtless we still hear of much misgovernment, and scandalous abuses sometimes are detailed, for the evils to be checked had been the growth of ages, and the vigilance of a single ruler, however strict, must have been oftentimes at fault.

Imperial provinces.

The remaining countries, called imperial provinces, were ruled by generals, called *legati*, or in some few cases by proctors only. They held office during the good pleasure of their master, and for longer periods often than the senatorial governors. There are signs that the imperial provinces were better ruled, and that the transference of a country to this class from the other was looked upon as a real boon, and not as an empty honor.

General character of the new *régime*.

Such in its chief features was the system of Augustus, the rudiments of the bureaucratic system which was slowly organized by later ages. This was his constructive policy, and on the value of this creative work his claims to greatness must be based. To the provinces the gain undoubtedly was great. His rule brought them peace and order and the essentials of good government. It left the local forms of self-rule almost untouched, and lightened, if it did not quite remove, the incubus of oppression which had so long tightened its grasp upon their throats. At Rome, too, the feeling of relief was keenly felt. Credit recovered with a rebound after the victory at Actium. Prices and the rate of interest fell at once. The secret adherents of the fallen cause began to breathe again more freely when they heard no mention of proscription; the friends of order learnt with joy that the era of anarchy was closed; rigid republicans found their jealous suspicions half-disarmed by the respect shown for the ancient forms and names, by the courtesy with which the Senate had been treated, and above all, perhaps, by the modest, unassuming manners of their prince. For he shunned carefully all outward pomp, moved about the streets almost unattended, sat patiently through the games and shows which the Romans passionately loved, went out to dinner readily when asked, and charmed men by his simple courtesy. He could bear plain speaking too, for a blunt soldier to whose petition he said that he was too busy to attend, told him to his face, that he had never said he was too busy to expose his own life for him in battle. The expenses of his household scarcely rose to the level of those of many a wealthy noble; he wore no clothes save those made for him by Livia and her women, and studiously avoided all profusion or extravagance. He tried also to spare his people's purses, for upon a journey he often passed through a town by night, to give the citizens no chance of proving their loyalty by costly outlay.

The homely manners of Augustus.

Liberal outlay for public objects.

But he spent his treasure lavishly for public ends. The public games and festivals provided by him were on a scale of magnificence quite unexampled; great sums were often spent in largess to the populace of Rome. In times of scarcity corn was sold in the capital below cost price, besides the vast quantities distributed in free doles among the poor. Noble senators of decayed fortunes were often pensioned, to enable them to live up to their rank. Costly buildings set apart for public uses, temples, baths, theatres, and aqueducts, rose rapidly on every side. His kinsmen, intimates, all whom his influence could move, vied with him in such outlay, and helped him to realize the boast of later days, "that he found a city of brick, and left one of marble in its place." The great roads in Italy and through the provinces were carefully repaired, and a postal system set on foot, confined, it is true, to official uses. Armed patrols marched along the roads, brigandage was forcibly put down, slave-gangs were inspected, and the abuses of times of violence redressed. In the capital itself, a police force was organized for the first time, intended mainly at the first for protection against fire, but soon extended and made permanent to secure peace and order in the streets, which for centuries the Republic had neglected. In distant countries, his fatherly care was shown in time of need, by liberal grants of money, to help public works, or repair the ravages of earthquakes. The interests of the legions also were consulted, but not at the expense of quiet citizens, as before. Vast sums were spent in buying up lands in the neighborhood of the great towns of Italy, where war or slow decay had thinned their numbers, in order at once to recruit the urban population, and supply the veterans with farms. Colonies were planted, too, beyond the seas, for the relief of the over-grown populace of Rome.

There was enough in such material boons to conciliate all classes through the Empire. The stiff-necked champions of the Republic had died upon the battle-field; a generation had grown up demoralized by years of anarchy, and few were left to mourn the loss of freedom. Few eyes could see what was one day to be apparent that the disguises and the insincerities of the new *régime* were full of danger; that to senator and office-bearer the paths of politics were strewn with snares; that in the face of a timid or suspicious ruler, it would be as perilous to show their fear as to make a brave show of independence. For a while they heard the familiar sounds of Senate, consul, and of tribune; they saw the same pageants as of old in daily life. Nor did they realize as yet, that liberty was gone forever, and that the ancient forms that passed before them were as empty of real life as the ancestral masks that moved along the streets to the noble Roman's funeral pyre.

Ready acquiescence in these changes.

From the imperial machinery we may next turn to the great men who helped possibly to create and certainly to work it. It was the singular good fortune of Augustus to secure the services of two ministers like Agrippa and Mæcenas, of different genius but equal loyalty of character.

The chief ministers of Augustus.

Marcus Vipsanius, surnamed Agrippa, had been, in early days, the school-fellow and intimate of Octavius. They were at Apollonia together studying the philosophy and art of Greece, when the tidings came that Cæsar had been murdered. They were together when the bold scheme was formed and the two youths set forth together to claim the heritage

Agrippa.

of Cæsar, and to strive for the empire of the world. To whom the initiative was due, we know not; but we do know that Agrippa's courage never wavered, though Octavianus seemed at times ready to falter and draw back. To the many-sided activity of Agrippa and to his unfailing resolution, the success of that enterprise seems mainly due. He was the great general of the cause that triumphed, the hero of every forlorn hope, and the knight-errant for every hazardous adventure in distant regions. His energy helped to win Perusia after stubborn siege; his quick eye saw in the Lucrine lake the shelter for the fleets that were to be manned and trained before they could hope to face Sextus Pompeius, the bold corsair chief, who swept the seas and menaced Rome with famine. Thanks to him again the victory of Actium was won, for the genius if not the courage of Octavianus failed him on the scene of battle.

His energy.

Whenever danger showed itself henceforth—in Gaul, in Spain, where the native tribes rose once more in arms; in Pontus, where one of the line of Mithridates unfurled the banner of revolt; on the shores of the Danube, where the Pannonians were stirring—no hand but Agrippa's could be trusted to dispel the gathering storms. We find in him not heroism alone but the spirit of self-sacrifice. Three times, we read, he refused the honors of a triumph. At a word he stooped to the lowest round of official rank, the ædileship, burdened as it was with the ruinous responsibilities of shows and festivals, and kept the Romans in good humor at a critical moment of the civil struggle. To win further popularity by the sweets of material well-being, the soldier forsook the camp and courted the arts of peace, busied himself with sanitary reforms, repaired

Self-sacrifice.

Public works.

the magnificent *cloacæ* of old Rome, constructed the splendid *thermæ* for the hot baths introduced from Eastern lands, built new aqueducts towering aloft upon the arches of the old, and distributed the pure water so conveyed to fountains in every quarter of the city, which were decorated with statues and columns of precious marbles to be counted by the hundred. Another sacrifice was called for—to divorce the daughter of Atticus, Cicero's famous friend, and drew nearer the throne by marrying the Emperor's niece, Marcella; and he obeyed from dutiful submission to his master, or from the ambitious hope to share the power which his sword had won. Soon it seemed as if his loyalty was to meet with its reward. Augustus was brought to death's door by sudden illness, and, in what seemed like his last hour, seized Agrippa's hand and slipped a ring upon the finger, as if to mark him out for his successor. But health returned again, and with it visible coolness towards Agrippa and increased affection for Marcellus, his young nephew.

Marries Marcella.

Agrippa resigned himself without a murmur, and lived in retirement a while at Lesbos, till the death of Marcellus and the warnings of Mæcenas pointed him out again as the only successor worthy of the Empire. Signs of discontent among the populace of Rome quickened the Emperor's desire to have his trusty friend beside him, and to draw him yet more closely to him he bade him put away Marcella, and gave him his own daughter Julia. Once more he obeyed in silence, and now might fairly hope to be rewarded for his patience and one day to mount into the weakly Emperor's place. But his lot was to be always second, never first. His strong frame, slowly weakened by hard

Retires to Lesbos.

Marries Julia.

campaigns and ceaseless journeys at full speed in every quarter of the world, gave way at last, and his career was closed while he seemed yet in his prime. In him Augustus lost a gallant soldier and unselfish friend, who is said, indeed, to have advised him after Actium to resign his power, but who certainly had done more than any other to set him up and to keep him on the pinnacle of greatness. It throws a curious light upon his story to read the comment on it in the pages of the naturalist, Pliny. He is speaking of the superstitious fancy that misery clouded the lives of all who were called Agrippa. In spite, he says, of his brilliant exploits he was no exception to the rule. He was unlucky in his wife Julia, who dishonored his good name; in his children, who died by poison or in exile; and unhappy also in bearing all his life what he calls the hard bondage of Augustus. The friend for whom he toiled so long and faithfully showed little tenderness of heart; the master whom he served had tasked his energies in every sphere, and called for many an act of self-devotion, but he had already looked coldly on his loyal minister, and he might at any moment weary of a debt he could not pay, and add another page to the long chronicle of the ingratitude of princes.

Dies (B.C. 12).

Remarks of Pliny about him.

Mæcenas, better known by his mother's name than that of Cilnius, his father, came from an Etruscan stock that had given a line of masters to Arretium. He was better fitted for the council chamber than the field of battle, for the delicate manœuvres of diplomacy than for the rough work of stormy times. During the years of civic struggle, and while the air was charged with thunder-clouds, we find him always, as the trusty agent of Octavianus, engaged on every

Mæcenas.

important mission that needed adroitness and address. His subtle tact and courtesies were tried with the same success upon Sextus Pompeius and on Antonius, when the confidence of each was to be won, or angry feelings charmed away, or the dangers of a coalition met. His honied words were found of not less avail with the populace of Rome, when scarcity and danger threatened and the masters of the legions were away. It seemed, indeed, after the Empire was once established that his political career was closed, for he professed no high ambition, refused to wear the gilded chains of office, or to rise above the modest rank of knighthood. He seemed content with his great wealth (how gained we need not ask), with the social charms of literary circles and the refinements of luxurious ease, of which the Etruscans were proverbially fond. But his influence, though secret, was as potent as before. He was still the Emperor's chief adviser, counselling tact and moderation, ready to soothe his ruffled nerves when sick and weary with the cares of State. He was still serving on a secret mission, and one that lasted all his life. Keenly relishing the sweets of peace and all the refined and social pleasures which a great capital alone can furnish, haunted by no high principles to vex his Sybaritic ease, and gifted with a rare facility of winning words, he was peculiarly fitted to influence the tone of Roman circles and diffuse a grateful pride in the material blessings of imperial rule. He could sympathize with the weariness of men who had passed through long years of civic strife and seen every cause betrayed by turns, and who craved only peace and quiet, with leisure to enjoy and to forget.

His diplomatic skill.

Avoided official rank,

but was the chief adviser of Augustus.

Influenced the tone of Roman circles

through the poets

Instinct or policy soon led him to caress the poets of the day, for their social influence might be great. Their epigrams soon passed from mouth to mouth; a well-turned phrase or a bold satire lingered in the memory long after the sound of the verses died away; and the practice of public recitations gave them at times something of the power to catch the public ear which journalism has had in later days. So from taste and policy alike Mæcenas played the part of patron of the arts and letters.

as their patron. Horace.

He used the fine point and wit of Horace to sing the praises of the enlightened ruler who gave peace and plenty to the world, to scoff meantime at high ambitions, and play with the memory of fallen causes. The social philosophy of moderation soothed the self-respect of men who were sated with the fierce game of politics and war, and gladly saw their indolent and skeptical refinement reflected in the poet's graceful words.

Virgil.

He used the nobler muse of Virgil to lead the fancy of the Romans back to the good old days, ere country life was deserted for the camp and city, suggested the subject of the Georgics to revive the old taste for husbandry and lead men to break up the waste land with the plough. He helped also to degrade that muse by leading it astray from worthier themes to waste its melody and pathos in the uncongenial attempt to throw a halo of heroic legend round the cradle of the Julian line. Other poets, too, Propertius, Tibullus, Ovid, paid dearly for the patronage which cramped their genius and befouled their taste, and in place of truer inspiration prompted chiefly amorous insipidities and senile adulation.

His domestic trials.

For himself his chief aim in later life seemed careless ease, but that boon fled away from him the more he wooed it. The Emperor eyed Terentia, his wife, too fondly, and the injured husband consoled himself with the best philosophy he could. But she was a scold as well as a coquette, and now drove him to despair with bitter words, now lured him to her side again, till their quarrels passed at length beyond the house and became the common talk of all the gossips of the town. As he was borne along the streets, lolling in his litter, in a dress loose with studied negligence, his fingers all bedecked with rings, with eunuchs and parasites and jesters in his train, men asked each other with a smile what was the last news of the fickle couple—were they married or divorced again? At last his nerves gave way and sleep forsook him. In vain he had recourse to the pleasures of the table which his Tuscan nature loved, to the rare wines that might lull his cares to rest, to distant orchestras of soothing music. In earlier days he had set to tuneful verse what Seneca calls the shameful prayer, that his life might still be spared when health and strength and comeliness forsook him. He lived long enough to feel the vanity of all his wishes. Nothing could cure his lingering agony of sleeplessness or drive the spectre of death from his bedside. But the end came at last. He passed away, and, loyal even in his death, he left the Emperor his heir.

Sleeplessness.

We have watched Augustus in his public life, and marked his measures and his ministers; it is time now to turn to his domestic circle and see what influences were about him there. The chief figure to be studied is Livia, his wife, who had been the object of his violent love while still married to Tiberius Nero, and had been forced to quit her reluctant husband for the home of the triumvir. She soon gained over him

Livia.

Sources of her influence over Augustus,

an influence that never wavered. Her gentle courtesies of manner, her wifely virtues never tainted by the breath of scandal, the homeliness with which she copied the grave matrons of old days who stayed at home and spun the wool to clothe their men, the discreet reserve with which she shut her eyes to her husband's infidelities, are the reasons given by herself, as we are told, when she was asked for the secret of her power. Quite insufficient in themselves, they may have helped to secure the ascendency which her beauty and her strength of character had won. The

and its nature.

gradual change that may be traced in the outward bearing of Augustus may be due partly to her counsels. Certainly she seemed to press patience and forbearance on him, and Dion Cassius at a later time puts into her mouth a pretty sermon on the grace of mercy when her husband's temper had been soured by traitorous plots. She was open-handed too in works of charity, brought up poor children at her own expense, and gave many a maid a marriage dower. Caligula, who knew her well, and had insight in his own mad way, called her "Ulysses in petticoats;" and the men

Suspicion of her sinister dealings

of her own day, it seems, thought her such a subtle schemer, that they credited her with acts of guile of which no evidence was produced. Dark rumors floated through the streets of Rome, and men spoke of her in meaning whispers, as death knocked again and again at the old man's doors and the favorites of the people passed away. It was her misfortune or her guilt that all who were nearest to the Emperor, all who stood between her son and the succession, died by premature and seemingly mysterious deaths. The young Marcellus, to whose memory Virgil raised the monument of his pathetic lines; the brave

Agrippa, cut off when all his hopes seemed nearest to fulfillment; two of Julia's children by Agrippa, within eighteen months of each other; all died in turn before their time, and all were followed to the grave by regrets and by suspicions that grew louder in each case. For Livia had had no children by Augustus. The fruit of her first marriage Drusus died in Germany, and Tiberius alone was left. The popular fancy, goaded by repeated losses, found it easy to believe that a ruthless tragedy was going on before their eyes, and that the chief actor was a mother scheming for her son, calmly sweeping from his path every rival that she feared. One grandson still was left, the youngest of Julia's children, Agrippa Postumus, who was born after his father's death. On him Augustus lavished his love awhile as the last hope of his race, adopted him even as his own; but soon he found, or was led to fancy, that the boy was clownish and intractable, removed him to Surrentum, and when confinement made him worse, to the island of Planasia. But one day pity or regret stole over the old man's heart: he slipped away quietly with a single confidant to see the boy, seemed to feel the old love revive again, and spoke as if he would restore him to his place at home. The one bystander told his wife the story, and she whispered it to Livia's ear. That witness died suddenly soon after, and his wife was heard to moan that her indiscretion caused his death. Then Livia dared no longer to wait, lest a dotard's fondness should be fatal to her hopes. Quietly she took her potent drugs to a favorite fig tree in a garden close at hand, then as they walked together later on offered him the poisoned figs and ate herself of the harmless ones that grew beside.

to secure the succession of Tiberius.

Treatment of Agrippa Postumus.

Story of Livia poisoning Augustus.

Such were the stories that were current at the time, too lightly credited perhaps from fear or hate, but noteworthy as reflecting the credulous suspicions of the people, and the fatality that seemed to haunt the household of the Cæsars. Of that family the two Julias yet remained alive, the wife and daughter of Agrippa; but they were pining in their lonely prisons, and their memory had almost passed away.

Julia. Her betrothals

The elder Julia was the child of Augustus by Scribonia. Betrothed while still in the nursery to a young son of Antonius, she was promised in jest to Cotison, a chieftain of the Getæ, and then to the nephew of the Emperor, Marcellus. At his death she passed, at the age of seventeen and with her the hopes of succession to Agrippa's house where an earlier wife was displaced to make room for her. Eleven years she lived with him, and when he died Tiberius must in his turn divorce the Agrippina whom he loved and take the widowed princess to his house. She had been brought up strictly, almost sternly by her father. Profligate as he had been himself in early life, his standard of womanly decorum was a high one, and he wished to see in Julia the austere dignity of the Roman matrons of old days. But she was readier to follow the examples of his youth than the disguises and hypocrisies of his later life. She scorned the modest homeliness of Livia and the republican simplicity of Augustus, aired ostentatiously her pride of race, and loved profusion and display. Once freed by marriage from the restraints of her father's home, she began a career of license unparalleled even for that age. She flung to the winds all womanly reserves, paraded often in her speech a cynical disdain for conventional restraints, and gathered round her the most reck-

and marriages.

Her extravagance and profligacy,

less of the youth of Rome, till her excesses became a scandal and a byword through the town. The Emperor was the last to know of his dishonored name. He had marked, indeed, with grave displeasure her love of finery and sumptuous living, had even destroyed a house which she built upon too grand a scale; but for years no one dared to tell him more, till at last some one, perhaps Livia, raised the veil, and the whole story of her life was known. He heard of her long career of guilty license, and how but lately she had roved at night through the city with her train of revellers and made the Forum the scene of her worst orgies, dishonoring with bold words and shameless deeds the very tribune where her father stood but yesterday to speak in favor of his stricter marriage laws. He was told, though with little show of truth, that she was plotting a still darker deed and urging her paramour to take his life. The blow fell very hardly on the father, and clouded all the peace of his last years. At first his rage passed quite from his control. Her desks were ransacked, her slaves were tortured, and all the infamous details poured out before the Senate. When he was told that Phœbe, the freed woman and confidant of Julia, had hung herself in her despair he answered grimly, "Would that I were Phœbe's father." Nothing but her death seemed likely to content him. Then came a change; he shut himself away from sight, and would speak of her no more. She was exiled to a cheerless island; and though the fickle people, and Tiberius even, pleaded for her pardon, she was at most allowed at Rhegium a less gloomy prison. There, in her despairing loneliness, she must have felt a lingering agony of retribution. She heard how the hand

at last made known to her father.

Her banishment (B. C. 2)

and misery.

of vengeance fell upon her friends and paramours, and harder still to bear, how child after child mysteriously died, and only two were left—Agrippa, thrust away from sight and pity on his petty island, and Julia, who had followed in her mother's steps, and was an exile and a prisoner like herself.

Such family losses and dishonors might well embitter the Emperor's last years; but other causes helped to deepen the gloom which fell upon him. Since Agrippa's death there was no general whom he could trust to lead his armies, no strong hand to curb the restless tribes of the half-conquered North, or roll back from the frontiers the tide of war. He sent his grandsons to the distant armies; but they were young and inexperienced, and firmer hands than theirs were needed to save the eagles from disgrace.

One great disaster at this time revealed the danger and sent a thrill of horror through the Empire. The German tribes upon the Gallic border had kept unbroken peace of late, and many of them seemed quite to have submitted to the Roman rule. A few years before, indeed, some hordes had dashed across the Rhine upon a plundering foray, and in the course of it had laid an ambush for the Roman cavalry, and driven them and Lollius, their leader, backward in confusion and disgrace. But that storm had rolled away again, and the tribes sent hostages and begged for peace. Roman influence seemed spreading through the North, as year by year the legions and the traders carried the arts of settled life into the heart of Germany. But in an evil hour Quintilius Varus was sent thither in command. The rule seemed too lax and the change too slow for his impatience, and he set himself to consoli-

Disasters in Germany.

Defeat of Lollius

date and civilize in hot haste. Discontent and disaffection spread apace, but Varus saw no danger and had no suspicions. The German chieftains, when their plots were laid, plied him with fair assurances of peace, lured him to leave the Rhine and march towards the Visurgis (Weser) through tribes that were all ready for revolt. Wiser heads warned him of the coming danger, but in vain. He took no heed, he would not even keep his troops together and in hand. At last the schemers, Arminius (Hermann) at their head, thought the time had come. They began the rising at a distance, and made him think it only a local outbreak in a friendly country; so they led him on through forest lands, then rose upon him on all sides in a dangerous defile. The legions, taken by surprise as they were marching carelessly, hampered with baggage and camp-followers, could make little head against their foes. They tried to struggle on through swamps and woods, where falling trees crushed them as they passed along, and barricades were piled by unseen hands, while wind and rain seemed leagued together for their ruin. Three days they stood at bay and strove to beat off their assailants, who returned with fresh fury to the charge. Then their strength or courage failed them. The more resolute spirits slew themselves with their own hands, and the rest sank down to die. Of three full legions few survived, and for many a year the name of that field of death—the Saltus Teutoburgiensis—sounded ominously in Roman ears.

and loss of Varus, with three legions. A. D. 9.

In the capital there was a panic for a while. A short time before they had heard the tidings that Pannonia was in revolt, and now came the news that Germany was all in arms, and, forcing the Roman lines, stripped as they were of their

Panic at Rome,

army of defence, might pour even into Italy, which seemed a possible, nay easy prey. The danger, indeed, was not so imminent. Tiberius, and after him Germanicus, maintained the frontier and avenged their soldiers; but the loss of *prestige* was very great, and the emperor felt it till his death. For months of mourning he would not trim his beard or cut his hair, and "Varus, give me back my legions!" was the moan men often heard him utter. He felt it the more keenly because soldiers were so hard to find. At the centre no one would enlist. In vain he appealed to their sense of honor, in vain he had recourse to stringent penalties; he was forced at last to enroll freemen and make up his legions from the rabble of the streets. He had seen long since with alarm that the population was decreasing, had re-stocked the dwindling country towns with colonists, had tried to promote marriage among all classes, had forced through a reluctant Senate the Lex Papia Poppæa by which celibacy was saddled with penal disabilities. But men noticed with a sneer that the two consuls after whom the law was named were both unmarried, and it was a hopeless effort to arrest such social tendencies by legislation. The central countries of the Empire could not now find men to fill the ranks. The veterans might be induced to forsake the little glebes of which they soon grew weary, but others would not answer to the call. Whole regions were almost deserted, and the scanty populations had little mind for war. So the distant provinces became the legions' recruiting-ground, and the last comers in the Empire must defend it.

and grief of the Emperor,

who can hardly levy soldiers,

except in the provinces.

Under the pressure of such public and domestic cares

we need not wonder that the Emperor became moody and morose, and that the unlovely qualities of earlier days began to re-appear. He shunned the gentle courtesies of social life, would be present at no festive gatherings, disliked even to be noticed or saluted. Increasing weakness gave him an excuse for failing to be present in the Senate—a few picked men could represent the body, and the Emperor's bed-chamber became a privy council. He heard with petulance that the exiles in the Islands were trying to relax the rigor of their lot, and living in comfort and in luxury. Stringent restrictions were imposed upon their freedom. He heard of writings that were passing through men's hands in which his name was spoken of with caustic wit and scant respect. The books must be hunted out at once and burnt, and the authors punished if they could be found. The bitter partisanship with which Titus Labienus had expressed his republican sympathies, and the meaning look with which he turned over pages of his history, which could be read only after he was dead, have made his name almost typical of the struggle between despotism and literary independence. Cassius Severus said he must be burnt himself, if the memory of Labienus' work must be quite stamped out; and his was, accordingly, the first of the long list of cases in which the old laws of treason—the *Leges Majestatis*—were strained to reach not acts alone but words. A much more familiar name, the poet Ovid, is brought before us at this time. The spoiled child of the fashionable society of Rome, he had early lent his facile wit to amuse the careless worldlings round him, had made a jest of the remonstrances of serious friends,

Augustus grew morose,

and resented criticism.

Leges Majestatis enforced against authors.

Ovid.

who tried to win his thoughts to politics and busy life, and had squandered all his high gifts of poetry on frivolous or wanton themes. His conversational powers or his literary fame attracted the notice of the younger Julia, and he was drawn into the gay circle that surrounded her. There in an evil hour, it seems, he was made the confidant of dangerous secrets, and was one of the earliest to suffer when the Emperor's eyes at last were opened. To the would-be censor and reformer of the public morals, who had turned his back upon the follies of his youth, the poet's writings must have been long distasteful, as thinly veiled allurements to licentiousness. The indignant grandfather eyed them still more sternly, saw in them the source or the apology of wanton deeds, and drove their author from the Rome he loved so well to a half-civilized home at Tomi, on the Scythian frontier, from which all his unmanly flatteries and lamentations failed him.

Banished to Tomi. A.D. 8.

It was time Augustus should be called away; he had lived too long for happiness and fame, his subjects were growing weary of their master, and some were ready to conspire against him. Still doubtless in the provinces men blessed his name, as they thought of the prosperity and peace which he had long secured to them. One ship's crew of Alexandria, we read, when he put into Puteoli, where they were, came with garlands, frankincense, and glad words of praise to do him honor. "To him they owed," so ran their homage, "their lives, their liberties, and the well-being of their trade." But those who knew him best were colder in their praises now, and scarcely wished that he should tarry long among them. For seventy-five years his strength held out, sickly and

Augustus at last less popular at Rome than in the provinces.

enfeebled as his body seemed. The summons came as he was coasting by Campania, and left him only time to crawl to Naples and thence to Nola, where he died. To those who stood beside his bed his last words, if reported truly, breathe the spirit of his life: "What think ye of the comedy, my friends? Have I fairly played my part in it? If so, applaud." The applause, if any, must be given to the actor rather than to the man, for the least lovely features of his character seem most truly his.

Died at Nola.

In his last years he was busy with the task of giving an account of his long stewardship. Long ago he had set on foot a survey of the Empire, and maps had been prepared by the geographical studies of Agrippa. Valuations of landed property had been made, as one step, though a very partial one, towards a uniform system of of taxation. He had now gathered up for the benefit of his successors and the Senate all the varied information that lay ready to his hand. He had written out with his own hand, we are told, the statistics of chief moment, an account of the population in its various grades of privilege, the muster-rolls of all the armies and the fleets, and the balance-sheet of the revenue and expenditure of state. Taught by the experience of later years, or from the depression caused by decaying strength, he added for future rulers the advice to be content with organizing what was won already, and not to push the frontiers of the army further. Before he died he took a last survey of his own life, wrote out a summary of all the public acts which he cared to recall to memory, and left directions that the chronicle should be engraved on brazen tablets in the

His survey of the Roman world,

and summary of official statistics,

and advice to his successors.

mausoleum built to do him honor. That chronicle may still be read, though not at Rome. In a distant province, at the town of Ancyra, in Galatia, a temple had been built for the worship of Augustus, and the guardian priests had a copy of his own biography carved out at length in stone on one of the side-walls. The temple has passed since then to other uses and witnessed the rites of a different religion; houses have sprung up round it, and partly hidden, though probably preserved, the old inscription. Until of late only a part of it could be deciphered, but a few years ago the patient energy of the explorers sent out by the French Government succeeded in uncovering the whole wall and making a complete copy of nearly all that had been written on it. From the place where it was found its literary name is the "Monumentum Ancyranum." It is not without a certain grandeur, which even those may feel who dispute the author's claim to greatness. With stately confidence and monumental brevity of detail it unfolds the long roll of his successes. Disdaining seemingly to stoop to the pettiness of bitter words, it speaks calmly of his fallen rivals; veiling, indeed, in constitutional terms the illegalities of his career, but misleading or unfair only by its silence. Not a word is there to revive the hateful memory of the proscriptions, little to indicate the dire suspense of the war with Sextus Pompeius, or the straits and anxieties of the long struggle with Antonius; but those questionable times of his career once passed, the narrative flows calmly on. It recounts with proud self-confidence the long list of battles fought and victories won; the nations finally subdued under his rule; the Eastern potentates who sought his friendship; the vassal princes who courted his protection. It tells of the many colonies which he

The Monumentum Ancyranum.

had founded, and of the towns recruited by its veterans; speaks of the vast sums that he had spent on shows and largess for the people; and describes the aqueducts and various buildings that had sprung up at his bidding to add to the material magnificence of Rome. For all these benefits the grateful citizens had hailed him as the father of his country. To the provincials who read these lines it might seem perhaps that there were few signs in them of any feeling that the Empire owed any duties to themselves. A few words of reference to the sums spent in time of need upon their towns, and that was all. To the administrator it might seem a strange omission to say nothing of the great change in the ruling mechanism. Yet in what was there omitted lay his claim to greatness. The plea which justified the Empire was found in the newly-organized machinery of government and in the peace and justice long secured to the whole civilized world.

Augustus deified.

Explanations.

High as he had risen in life, he was to be raised to a yet higher rank after his death, and the deified Augustus became, like many a succeeding emperor, the object of a national worship. A phenomenon so startling to our modern thought calls for some words of comment. First, we may note that polytheism naturally tends to efface the boundary-lines between the human and the divine. It peoples earth and air and water with its phantom beings, of bounded powers and clashing wills, and weaves with wanton hand the fanciful tissue of its legends, in which it plays with the story of their loves and hates and fitful moods of passion, till its deities can scarcely be distinguished from the mortal men and women in whose likeness they are pictured.

1. Polytheism less scrupulous.

Eastern thought, moreover, seldom scrupled to honor its great men with the names and qualities of godhead. Often in servile flattery, sometimes perhaps in the spirit of a mystic creed, it saw in the rulers whom it feared a sort of *avatar* or incarnation of a power divine, which it made the object of its worship. The Pharaohs of Egypt and the monarchs of Assyria were deified in their lifetime by the language of inscriptions, and in later times temples were raised in Asia Minor in honor of the governors of the day, so that Antonius and Cleopatra gave little shock to Eastern sentiment when in their royal pageant they assumed the titles and symbols of Isis and Osiris. It was, therefore, on this side of the Roman world that the fashion of worshipping the Emperor began. Even in the lifetime of Augustus deputations came from towns of Asia which were anxious to set up altars and build temples in his honor. For awhile, indeed, he treated them with coldness and sometimes with mockery, he yet could not quite repress the enthusiasm of their servile worship, which grew apace in the more distant provinces.

2. Eastern peoples had deified their kings.

Less credulous minds looked upon the tendency as only a fanciful way of symbolizing a great fact. Much of the simple faith in the old legendary creeds had passed away before the critical spirit of Greek culture, and many thought that the heroes and gods of the old fables were but the great men of past times seen through the mist of popular fancy, till a divine halo gathered round their superhuman stature. If the sentiment of bygone days had made gods out of the men who sowed the seeds of art and learning and tamed the savagery of early life, the wondering awe of ignorant folk might be allowed to crystalize still in the same forms, and to find a national

3. The rationalizing tendency, or euhemerism.

deity in the great ruler who secured for the whole world the boon of civilized order. So reasoned probably the critical and unimpassioned, content to humor the credulous fancy of the masses, and to deal tenderly with an admiration which they did not share, but which it might be dangerous to thwart.

4. The Italian worship of the Lares

Above all, in Italy the tendency in question found support and strength in a widespread feeling which had lingered on from early times, that the souls of men did not pass away at death, but still haunted their old homes, and watched as guardian Lares over the weal and woe of the generations that came after. Offering and prayer seemed but a fitting token of respect, and might be useful to quicken their sympathies or appease their envy. Thus every natural unity, the family, the clan, the canton, and the nation, had their tutelary powers and special ritual of genuine home-growth, while nearly all besides the foreign influences had overlaid the old religious forms. It had been part of the conservative policy of Augustus to foster these old forms of worship, to repair the little chapels in the city wards, and to give priestly functions to the *masters of the streets* officially connected with them. Even while he lived he allowed the figure of his Genius to be placed in the chapels beside the Lares. At his death divine honors were assigned to it as to the rest, or rather it rose above them all, as the imperial unity had towered above the petty districts which they were thought to guard. Temples rose to the deified Augustus, altars smoked in every land, and guilds of Augustales were organized to do him priestly service—for the provinces were eager to follow the example of the imperial city, and

especially fostered by Augustus.

The Genius of Augustus.

Augustales.

their loyal zeal had even outstripped the reverence of Rome. The ruling powers were well pleased to see a halo of awfulness gather round their race, while subject people saw in the apotheosis of the monarch only a fitting climax to the majesty of his life and a symbol of the greatness of the Empire. And so succeeding monarchs in their turn were deified by pagan Rome, as saints were canonized by favor of the Pope. The Senate's vote gave divine honors with the title of "Divus," and it was passed commonly as a matter of course, or withheld only as a token of abhorrence or contempt.

CHAPTER II.

TIBERIUS.—A.D. 14–37.

The early life of Tiberius.

TIBERIUS CLAUDIUS NERO was the son of Tiberius Nero and Livia, and was carried by them while still an infant in their hurried flight after the surrender of Perusia. On their return to Rome after the general peace his parents were separated by the imperious will of Octavianus, who made Livia his wife. Losing his father at the age of nine, and taken from the nursery to pronounce the funeral speech, he was placed again under his mother's care and became the object of her ambitious hopes. He married the daughter of Agrippa, and loved her well, but was forced to leave her afterwards for Julia, who brought as her dowry the prospects of the imperial succession. He was soon sent to learn the business of a soldier, serving in the campaign in Pannonia and Germany, and dispatched on missions of

Service in the field

importance, such as to crown Tigranes in Armenia as a subject prince, and to carry home the eagles which had been lost in Parthia by Crassus. At home all the old offices of State were pressed upon him, till at last he was honored even with the significant honor of the tribunician power.

and in offices of State.

Yet Augustus seems to have had little liking for him, and to have noted keenly all his faults, the taciturn sullenness which contrasted painfully with the Emperor's gayer moods, his awkward gestures and slow articulation when he spoke, the haughtiness of manner which came naturally to all the Claudian line, and the habit of hard drinking, on which the rude soldiers spent their wit when they termed him punningly "Biberius Nero." The Emperor even went so far as to speak to the Senate on the subject, and to say that they were faults of manner rather than of character. For the rest we hear that he was comely in face and well-proportioned, and handsome enough to attract Julia's fancy; nor could he be without strong natural affection, for he loved his first wife fondly, and lived happily with Julia for awhile, and showed the sincerest sorrow when his brother Drusus died. This is all we hear of him till the age of thirty-five. Then comes a great break in his career. Suddenly, without a word of explanation, he wishes to leave Rome and retire from public life. Livia's entreaties, the Emperor's protests, and the remonstrances of friends have no effect; and having wrung from Augustus his consent, he betakes himself to Rhodes. What were his motives cannot now be known. It may have been in part his disgust at the guilty life of Julia, who outraged his honor and allowed her paramours to make merry with his character;

Little liked by Augustus.

His retirement to Rhodes (B.C. 6)

in part perhaps weariness at being always kept in leading-strings at Rome; but most probably it was jealousy at the rising star of the young grandsons of the Emperor, and fear of the danger that might flow from too visible a rivalry. In the pleasant isle of Rhodes he lived awhile, quietly enough, though he could not always drop his rank. One day he was heard to say that he would go and see the sick. He found that he was saved the trouble of going far in search, as the magistrates had them all brought out and laid in order under the arcades, with more regard to his convenience than theirs. Another time, when a war of words was going on among the wranglers in the schools, he stepped into the fray, and was so much hurt at being roughly handled that hurrying home, he sent a guard to seize the poor professor who had ventured to ignore his dignity. At length, growing weary of his stay at Rhodes, he said that the young princes were now secure of the succession, and that he might safely take a lower place at Rome. But Augustus coldly bade him stay and take no further trouble about those whom he was so determined to forsake.

where he lives quietly though with occasional show of power.

He wished to return to Rome, but was not allowed.

Then came a time of terrible suspense. He knew that he was closely watched, and that the simplest words were easily misjudged. The Emperor reproached him with tampering with the loyalty of the officers who put in at Rhodes to see him. He shunned the coast and lived in solitude, to avoid all official visits, and yet he heard to his alarm that he was still regarded with suspicion, that threatening words had passed about him in the intimate circle of the young Cæsars, that his prospects looked so black that the citizens of Nemausus (Nismes) had even flung his statue

His danger and suspense.

down to curry favor with his enemies, that his innocence would help him little, and that at any moment he might fall. Only Thrasyllus, his astrologer, might see him, to excite him with ambiguous words. But Livia's influence was strong enough at last to bring him back to Rome, after more than seven years of absence to live, however, in complete retirement, in the gardens of Mæcenas, to take like a school-boy to mythology, and pose the grammarians who formed his little court with nice questions about the verses which the Sirens used to sing, or the false name which the young Achilles bore. Not until the death of the young Cæsars was he taken back to favor and adopted by the Emperor as his son.

Livia procured his recall (A. D. 2.)

and adoption by Augustus.

But the weariness of those long years of forced inaction, the lingering agony of that suspense had done their work, and he resigned himself henceforth without a murmur to the Emperor's will. Not a moment of impatience at the caprices of the sick old man, not an outspoken word nor hasty gesture now betrayed his feelings; but, as an apt pupil in the school of hypocrisy about him, he learned to dissemble and to wait. The only favor that he asked was to take his post in every field of danger, and to prove his loyalty and courage. With all his powers of self-restraint he must have breathed more freely in the camp than in the stifling air of Rome, and the revolt in Pannonia gave him the opportunity he needed. That war, said to be the most dangerous since the wars with Carthage, tasked for three years all his resources as a general at the head of fifteen legions. Scarcely was it closed when the defeat of Varus summoned him to the German frontier to avenge the terrible disaster. In the

His patient self-control henceforth.

Was usually away from Rome with the army.

campaigns that followed he spared no vigilance or personal effort, shared the hardships of the soldiers, and enforced the rigorous discipline of ancient generals. Not only does Velleius Paterculus, who served among his troops, speak of his commander in terms of unbounded praise, but later writers, who paint generally a darker picture, describe his merits at this time without reserve.

Recalled to the death-bed of Augustus.

From such duties he was called away to the death-bed of Augustus, whom he found at Nola, either dead already or almost at the last gasp. But Livia had been long since on the watch, had strictly guarded all approach to his bed-side, and let no one know that the end was near till her son was ready and their measures had been taken.

Precautions of Livia.

He had been long since marked out for the succession by the formal act of adoption, which made him the natural heir, as also by the partnership in the tribunician dignity, which raised him above all the other subjects.

Claim to succeed based on adoption and tribunicia potestas.

But the title to the sovereign rank was vague and ill-defined, and no constitutional theory of succession yet existed. As the Empire by name and origin rested on a military basis the consent of the soldiery was all-important.

Consent of the legions all-important.

If the traditions of many years were to have weight, the Senate must be consulted and respected. The legions were far away upon the frontiers, in greatest force upon the side of Germany and Pannonia; and the first news that came from the North was that the two armies were in mutiny, clamoring for higher pay and laxer discipline.

They were in mutiny,

The hasty levies raised after the defeat of Varus had lowered the general *morale*, and carried to the camp the turbulent license of the capital. On the Rhine there was the further danger that Germanicus, his nephew, who was then in supreme command, should rely on his influence with his troops and lead them on, or be led by them, to fight for empire. This son of Drusus, who had been the popular idol of his day, and who was said to have hankered after the old liberties of the Republic, had won himself the soldiers' hearts by his courtesy, gallantry and grace, and the familiar name of Germanicus which they gave him is the only one by which history has known him since. They were ready to assert their right to be consulted. The power which they defended was in their hands to give at a word from him, and if that word had been spoken they would certainly have marched in arms to Rome. But he was not fired by such ambitious hopes, nor had he seemingly any sentimental dreams of ancient freedom. He took without delay the oath of obedience to Tiberius, restored discipline after a few anxious days of mutiny, and then tried to distract the thoughts of his soldiers from dangerous memories by a series of campaigns into the heart of Germany.

and were ready to raise Germanicus to the highest rank,

had he been willing.

Tiberius meanwhile at home was feeling his way with very cautious steps. While he was still uncertain of the attitude of Germanicus and the temper of the legions, he used nothing but ambiguous language, affected to decline the reins of the state, kept even the Senate in suspense, and at last with feigned reluctance accepted office only for awhile, till they should see fit to give him rest. It was in keeping with such policy that he shrank from the excessive honors which the Senate

Caution of Tiberius and ambiguous language.

Shrank from titles of honor

and from flattery.

tried to lavish on him, and declined even the titles which Augustus had accepted. Either from fear or from disgust he showed dislike to the flattery which was at first rife about him, checked it when it was outspoken, and resented even as a personal offence the phrases "lord" and "master" as applied to him.

Referred all business to the Senate,

Meantime the Senate was encouraged to think that the powers of administration rested in their hands. Nothing was too paltry, nothing was too grave to be submitted for their discussion; even military matters were at first referred to them, and generals in command were censured for neglecting to report their doings to the Council. The populace of Rome, however, was treated with less courtesy. The ancient forms of the elections were quite swept away, and in legislation also the Senate took the place of the popular assembly. Little attempt was made to keep the people in good humor by shows of gladiators or gorgeous pageants, and Tiberius would not try to put on the studied affability with which Augustus sat for hours through the spectacles, or the frank courtesy with which he stayed to salute the passers by. But, on the other hand, he showed himself at first sincerely desirous of just rule, warned provincial governors who pressed him to raise higher taxes that "a good shepherd shears but does not flay his sheep," and kept a careful watch on the tribunals to see that the laws were properly enforced. Vigorous measures were adopted to put down brigandage, the police of Italy was better regulated, popular disturbances in the capital or in the provinces were promptly and even sternly checked, and many of the abuses were remedied which had grown out of the old rights of sanctuary.

but neglected the popular assemblies and the amusements of the people.

Seemed anxious to govern well.

The policy of the early years of the new reign must have been largely due to Livia's influence. For many years Tiberius had been much away from Rome, and it was natural that he should at first rely upon his mother's well-tried statecraft, her knowledge of men and familiar experience of the social forces of the times. He owed all to her patient scheming, even if she had not, as men thought, swept away by poison the obstacles to his advancement. Her position was for many reasons a commanding one. The will of Augustus had named her as co-heiress, given her the official title of Augusta, and raised her by adoption to the level of her son. She shared with him, therefore, in some measure the imperial dignity; their mames were coupled in official language; the letters even of Tiberius ran for some time in her name as well as his. There were numerous coins of local currency, at Rome and in the provinces, on which her name was stamped, sometimes joined with her son's but oftener alone. At her bidding, or by her influence, priesthoods were formed and temples rose in all parts of the empire to extend the worship of the deified Augustus; and inscriptions still preserved upon them testify to her pride of self-assertion, as well as to the policy with which she strove to surround the imperial family with the solemn associations of religious awe. To that end she also enlisted the fine arts in her service, and found employment for the first sculptors, engravers and painters of the day in multiplying copies of the features of the ruling race, and endearing them to the imagination of the masses.

The great influence of Livia,

now called Augusta.

Her politic patronage of art.

The Senate was not slow to encourage the ambition of Augusta. Vote after vote was passed as the members tried to outdo each other in their flattery, till they raised her even to the foremost place, and proposed to call the Emperor Livius to do her honor. Tiberius, indeed, demurred to this; and before long there were signs clear enough to curious eyes that he was ashamed to feel he owed her all, impatient of her tutelage, and jealous of her high pretensions. Men spoke in meaning whispers to each other, and wits made epigrams on the growing coldness between mother and son. They said he vainly strove to keep her in the shade. Old as she was, she clung to power and state, and relied on her talents and influence to hold her own. The Senate and the camp she could not visit, but in all else she claimed to rule. As he seemed to shun the eyes of men she came forward more in public, won popular favor by her courtesies and generous gifts, gathered her crowd of courtiers round her, conferred at her will the offices of state, and tried to overawe the courts of justice when the interests of her favorites were at stake. In the circle of her intimates we hear of irreverent wits whose caustic speeches did not spare the Emperor himself; and once, we read, when words ran high between Augusta and her son, she took from her bosom old letters of Augustus and read sarcastic passages that bore on his faults of manner or of temper. This coolness did not lead to open rupture, for his old habits of obedience were confirmed enough to bear the strain, and he submitted to her claims, though grudgingly and ungraciously enough.

Tiberius showed jealousy of the honor paid to Augusta.

Coolness in their relations, but no open rupture.

She used her influence wisely on the whole,

On the whole she used her influence wisely, and while she ruled, the policy of state was cool and wary. She could be stern and resolute enough when force seemed needful. She had given orders for the death of Agrippa Postumus as soon as his grandfather had ceased to breathe. She did not plead for pity with her son when he let Julia die a wretched death of slow starvation in her prison, and took at last his vengeance on her paramour for the mockery and outrage of the past. It is likely even that her quick eye saw the use that might be made of the old laws of treason, which had come down from the Commonwealth. They had been meant to strike at men who had by open act brought dishonor or disaster on the state. Sulla was the first to make them cover libellous words, and Augustus had, though sparingly, enforced them in like cases. The Cæsar had already stepped into the people's place and screened his majesty against so-called treason; but when the Cæsar had been deified, any crime against his person was heightened by the sin of sacrilege. In the language of the law obedience to the living Emperor soon became confounded with the religious worship of the dead, and loyalty became in theory a sort of adoration. Any disrespect might carry danger with it. Jesting words against the late Emperor might be construed into blasphemy when the Emperor had become a god. His likeness must be held in honor, and it might be fatal even to beat a slave who clung for safety to his statue, or to treat carelessly his effigy upon a coin. A few such cases were enough to increase enormously the imperial *prestige*, and extend to the living members of the family some of the reverence that was gathering round the dead. But though Augusta had few scruples she had no taste for needless bloodshed, and while she lived she certainly exercised a restraining influence upon her son.

though she could be stern,

and perhaps suggested the new u-e of the "leges majestatis."

Another of the Emperor's family exerted a force of like restraint though in a very different way. Germanicus was the darling of the legions, and might at any moment be a pretender to the throne. He had calmed his mutinous soldiery, led them more than once into the heart of Germany, visited the battle-field where Varus fell, and brought back with him in triumph the captive wife and child of Arminius, the national hero of the Germans. It might seem dangerous to leave him longer at the head of an army so devoted to their general—dangerous perhaps to bring him back to win the hearts of men at Rome. But his presence might be useful in the East, for the kingdoms of Parthia and Armenia had been torn by civil war and thrown into collision by the claims of rival candidates for power, and by wars of succession due in part at least to the intrigues of Rome. A general of high repute was needed to protect the frontier and appease the neighboring powers, and the death of some of the vassal kings of Asia Minor had left thrones vacant, and wide lands to be annexed or organized. It was resolved to recall Germanicus from his post and to despatch him to the Syrian frontier on this important mission. On the north there was little to be gained by border warfare, which provoked but could not crush the resistance of the German tribes, and there was wisdom in following the counsel of Augustus not to aim at farther conquests. Germanicus might be unwilling to retire; but the duties to which he was transferred were of high dignity and trust. Yet men noted with alarm that Silanus who was linked to him by ties of marriage, was recalled from Syria at the time, and the haughty, self-willed Cnæus Piso made governor in his stead.

Restraining force exerted by the fear of Germanicus,

who was recalled from Germany,

and sent on a mission to the East.

The ominous appointment of Cn. Piso to be governor of Syria.

Dark rumors spread abroad that he had been chosen for the task of watching and of thwarting the young prince, and that his wife, Plancina, had been schooled in all the petty jealousies and spite of which Agrippina was the mark. So far at least all was mere suspicion, but there was no doubt that when they went to Syria the attitude of Piso was haughty and offensive. He made a bold parade of independence, disputed the authority and cavilled at the words and actions of Germanicus, tampered even with the loyalty of the soldiers, and drove him at last to open feud. When Germanicus fell ill soon afterwards Piso showed indecent glee, and though he was on the eve of quitting Syria he lingered till further news arrived. He put down by violence the open rejoicing of the crowd at Antioch when cheerful tidings came. Still he waited and the murmur spread that the sickness was his work, and that poison and witchcraft had been used to gratify his spite and perhaps to do the Emperor's bidding. Germanicus himself was ready to believe the story and to fear the worst. Suspicions gained force as he grew weaker, and his last charge on his death-bed to his friends was to expose his murderer and avenge his death. The sad story was received at Rome with passionate sorrow and resentment. His father's memory, his noble qualities and gentle bearing, had endeared him to all classes, and men recalled the ominous words that "those whom the people love die early." One after another their favorites had passed away, cut off in the spring-time of their youth; and now the last of them, the best beloved perhaps of all, had been sent away from them, they murmured, to the far East to die from the noxious air of Syria, or it might be from the virulence of Piso's hate.

His offensive conduct to Germanicus,

who believed that he was poisoned by Piso. A. D. 19.

Passionate grief at Rome when his death was known.

Still more outspoken was the grief when the chief mourners reached the shores of Italy, and passed in sad procession through the towns. At the sight of the widowed Agrippina, and the children gathered round the funeral urn that held his ashes, all classes of society vied with each other in the tokens of their sympathy. There was no flattery in such signs of mourning, for few believed that Tiberius was sorry, and many thought that he was glad at the loss that they regretted. Was it grief that kept him in the palace, or fear lest men should read his heart? Was it due respect to his young nephew to give such scant show of funeral honors, and to frown at the spontaneous outburst of his people's sorrow? Was it love of justice or a sense of guilt that made him so slow to punish Piso's crime, so quick to discourage the zeal of his accusers? They could only murmur and suspect, for nothing certain could be known. At Piso's trial there was evidence enough of angry words and bitter feelings, of acts of insubordination, almost of civil strife, but no proof that Germanicus was murdered, still less that Tiberius was privy to the deed. It was, indeed, whispered abroad that the accused had evidence enough to prove that he only did what he was bidden; but if so, he feared to use it, and before the trial was over he died by his own hand.

Popular suspicions,

but no proof of foul play.

The popular suspicion against Tiberius was no mere after-thought of later days, when Rome had learnt to know the darker features of his character. From the first they had never loved him, and the more they saw the less they liked him. He seemed of dark and gloomy temper, with no grace or geniality of manner, shunning the pleasures of the people, and

The people disliked Tiberius from the first.

Reasons.

seldom generous or open-handed. He had even an ungracious way of doing what was right, and spoiled a favor by his way of granting it. There was such reserve and constraint in what he said that men thought him a profound dissembler and imputed to him crimes he had no thought of. They seemed to have divined the cruelty that was still latent, and to have detested him before his acts deserved their hate. Even in the early years the satires current in the city and the epigrams passed from mouth to mouth show us how intense was the dislike ; and soon we see enough to justify it.

One of the most alarming features of the times in which men traced his influence was the rapid spread of professional accusers, of the *delatores*, of whom we read, indeed, before, but who now became a power in the state. The Roman law of early times looked to private citizens to expose wrong-doing, and to impeach civil or political offenders. Sometimes it was a moral indignation, oftener it was the bitterness of party feeling, and oftener still the passion of ambition, that brought them forward as accusers. The great men of the Republic were constantly engaged in legal strife. Cato, for example, was put on his defence some four-and-forty times, and appeared still oftener as accuser. It was commonly the first step in a young man's career to single out a prominent member of the rival party, to charge him with some political offence, and to prove in the attack his courage or knowledge of the laws. This practice naturally intensified the bitterness of party struggles, and often led to family feuds. It took to some extent the place of the duelling of modern times, and led more than once to a sort of hereditary "vendetta." It oftener served the passions of a party than the real

The "delatores" of the Empire now first appeared.

Common practice of impeachment under the Republic.

interests of justice; and, prized as it was as a safeguard and privilege of freedom, fostered license more than liberty. Yet, as if this tendency were not strong enough already, measures were taken to confirm it. More sordid motives were appealed to, and hopes of money bribes were held out to spur on the accuser's zeal. These, it may be, seemed more needful, as moral sympathies were growing stronger and the party passions of the Commonwealth were cooling down. Certainly the meaner motives must have been most potent in the days of the early Empire, when men came forward to enforce the sumptuary and marriage laws which were almost universally disliked.

Rewards offered to stimulate the zeal of informers.

We hear little of the *delatores* as a class under Augustus; but in the days of his successor they became almost at once of prominent importance. The wider range given to the laws of treason, the vagueness of the crimes that fell within their scope, and the terror of the penalties that threatened the accused, armed the informers with a class of weapons which they had not known before. With a ruler like Tiberius they became quite a new wheel in the political machinery. It suited his reserve to keep himself in the background while the objects of his fear or his suspicions were attacked, to learn the early stages of the trial from men who had no official connection with himself, while the Senate or the law courts were responsible for the result, and he could step in at last to temper, if he pleased, the rigor of the sentence. He did not own them for his instruments, refused even to speak to them directly on the subject; but with instinctive shrewdness they interpreted his looks, divined his wishes, and acted with eagerness

Their influence under Tiberius,

upon a word that fell from any confidant whom he semed to trust. No wonder that their numbers grew apace, for it seemed an easy road to wealth and honor. Settling even by threes and fours upon their victims, they disputed the precedence of the attack, for if they were successful the goods of the condemned might be distributed among them; and when an enemy of Cæsar fell, quite a shower of official titles, was rained upon them. They came from all classes alike. Some there were of ancient lineage and good old names; some were adventurers from the provinces who had come to push their fortunes in the capital; some even of the meanest rank who crowded into a profession where a ready tongue and impudence seemed the only needful stock in trade. For all were trained in early youth to speak and plead and hold their own in the keen fence of words. In the days of the Republic all must learn to speak who would make their way in public life, and the training of the schools remained the same when all besides was changed around them. The orator's harangues had been silenced in the Forum. No Cicero might hope to sway the crowd or guide the Senate, but they disputed still and declaimed and labored at the art of rhetoric as if oratory were the one end and aim of life. When life opened on them in real earnest they soon discovered how slowly honest and unaided talent could hope to make its way to fame. The conditions of the times were changed, and one only way was left to copy the great orators of earlier days. They could yet win wealth and honor, and make the boldest spirits quail, and be a power in the State, and gain perhaps the Emperor's favor, by singling out some man of mark, high in office

and increase in numbers.

Early training in oratory still common,

though of little use in most careers,

but useful to the informers,

or in rank, and furbishing afresh against him the weapons drawn from the armory of the laws of treason. If they were not weighted with nice scruples, if they could work upon the ruler's fears or give substance to his vague suspicions; if they were dexterous enough to rake up useful scraps of evidence and put their lies into a telling form, then they might hope to amass great fortunes speedily and to rise to high official rank. Did any wish to pay off an old debt of vengeance, or to force a recognition from the classes that despised them, or to retrieve a shattered fortune and to find a royal road to fame, it needed only to swell the ranks of the reformers, to choose a victim and invent a crime. If no plausible story could be found to ruin him, it was always possible to put into his mouth some threats against the Emperor's life, some bold lampoon upon his vices, which they found all ready to their hand. The annals of the times are full of tales which show how terrible was the power they wielded. Through every social class and circle the poison of suspicion spread, for every friend might prove a traitor and be an informer in disguise. It might be perilous to speak about affairs of State, for the frankest words of confidence might be reported, and be dangerously misconstrued. It might be dangerous to be too silent, for fear of being taken for a malcontent. A man's worst enemies might be in his home, for every house was full of slaves, who learned or guessed the master's secrets, and whose eyes were always on the watch to divine the inmost feelings of his heart. In a few minutes, by a few easy words, they could wreak their vengeance for the slights of years, gain their freedom even by their master's death, and with it such a slice of what was his as would make them rich beyond their wildest dreams. No inno-

who became objects of terror,

and caused widespread mistrust

cence could be quite secure against such foes, for it was as easy to invent as to report a crime. No council-chamber was so safe but that some traitorous ear could lurk unseen, for in one trial it appeared that three senators were hidden between the ceiling and the roof to hear the conversation of the man whom they accused. There was no kind of life without its dangers. To eschew politics was not enough. The poet's vanity might lure him to his ruin if he ventured to compose an elegy upon the prince's son, when the noble subject of his verse was sick, not dead. The historian's life might pay the penalty for a few bold words of freedom, as Cremutius Cordus had to die for calling the murderers of Cæsar the last of the old Romans. Philosophy itself might be suspected, for a lecture on the "whole duty of man" might recognize another standard than the Emperor's will and pleasure, and handle his special faults too freely. There was no escape from dangers such as these. In earlier days men might leave Rome before the trial was quite over, and shun the worst rigor of the law by self-chosen banishment from home. But the strong arm of the imperial ruler could reach as far as the farthest limits of the empire, and flight seemed scarcely possible beyond. One only road of flight lay open, and to that many had recourse. When the fatal charges had been laid, men often did not stay to brook the ignominy of the trial, or face the informer's torrent of invectives, but had their veins opened in the bath, or by poison or the sword ended the life which they despaired to save. They hoped to rescue by their speedy death some little of their fortune for their children, and to secure at least the poor advantage of a decent funeral for their bodies.

and danger,

from which there was no escape,

except in suicide.

It was the Emperor's suspicious temper that increased so largely the influence of the *delatores;* but there was one man who gained his trust, and gained it only to abuse it. Lucius Ælius Sejanus had long since won favor by artful insight into character and affected zeal and self-devotion. His flattery was too subtle to offend, his duplicity so skilful as to mask completely his own pride and ambition, while he fed the watchful jealousy of his master by whispered doubts of others. His father, a knight of Tuscan stock, had been præfect of the imperial guards, ten battalions of which were quartered in different places round the city. When the son was raised to the same rank, his first act of note was to induce the Emperor to concentrate the guards in one camp near the gates, as the permanent garrison of Rome. That done, he spared no pains to win the good-will of the soldiers, to secure the devotion of the officers, and raise his tools to posts of trust. To the real power thus secured, the rapidly increasing favor of Tiberius lent visible authority. In official language he was sometimes named as the partner of the ruler's labors; senators and nobles of old family courted his patronage with humble words; official titles were bestowed at his discretion, and spies and informers speedily were proud to take rank in his secret service. While ambitious hopes were growing within him with the self-confidence of a proud and resolute nature, the passion of revenge came in to define and to mature them. Drusus, the young son of Tiberius, whom we read of as coarse, choleric, and cruel, happened in a brawling mood to strike Sejanus on the face. The blow was one day to be washed out in blood, but for the moment it was borne in

The character of Sejanus.

His rise in power and favor.

He schemed to revenge himself on Drusus for the insult of a blow.

silence. He made no sign to rouse suspicion, but turned to Livilla, the prince's wife, and plied her with his wily words, seconded by winning grace and personal beauty. The weak woman yielded to the tempter. Flinging away her womanly honor, and with it tenderness and scruple, she sacrificed her husband to her lover. With her help he had Drusus poisoned, and so removed the heir presumptive to the throne.

Seduced Livilla, and poisoned Drusus,

Next came the turn of Agrippina and her children. Between the widowed mother and Tiberius a certain coolness had grown up already, which it was easy to increase. Her frank, impetuous, high-souled nature could not breathe freely in the palace. Proud of her husband's memory and the promise of her children, and too reliant on the people's love, she could not stoop to weigh her words, to curb her feelings, and school herself to be wary and submissive. His dark looks and freezing manner stung her often to impatience, and she allowed herself to show too clearly the want of sympathy between them. The ill-timed warmth of Agrippina's friends, the dark insinuations of Sejanus, widened the breach already made, and each was made to fear the other and hint at poison or at treason. The thunder-clouds had gathered fast, and the storm would soon have burst between them, had not Augusta stayed his hand and stepped in with milder counsels. Jealous as he may have been, the son still submitted to the mother's sway. He feared an open rupture, while he chafed at her interference and restraint. Then the schemer thought of parting them. Away from Rome and from his mother, Tiberius would breathe more freely, and lean more on his trusted servant, and

and widened the breach between Tiberius and Agrippina,

and urged Tiberius to leave Rome and Augusta.

he himself also could mature his plans more safely if he were not always watched by that suspicious eye. For twelve years the Emperor had scarcely left the city; but he was weary at last of moving in the same round of public labors, of meeting always the same curious eyes, full as it seemed of fear or of mistrust.

The counsels of Sejanus took root and bore their fruit in season. At first Rome only heard that its ruler was travelling southward, then that he was at Capreæ, the picturesque island in the bay of Naples which had tempted Augustus with its charms and passed by purchase into his estates. Soon, they thought, he would be back again, but time went on and still he came not; and though he talked at times of his return, and came twice almost within sight, he never set foot within their walls again.

Tiberius retired to Capreæ, A.D. 26.

After three years he heard at Capreæ of his mother's death, but he was not present at her funeral, long neglected even to give the needful orders, and set at nought the last wishes of her will. Her death removed the only shield of Agrippina and her children. One after another their chief adherents had been swept away. The old generals that loved them had been struck down by the informers; the relentless jealousy of the Emperor and Sejanus had for years set spies upon them to report and exaggerate unguarded words. All the charges which had been gathered up meantime were at once laid before the Senate in a message full of savage harshness; the mother and her two eldest children were hurried off to separate prisons, with litters closed, lest the memory of Germanicus should stir the people. They languished there awhile, then perished miserably by sword and famine.

The death of Augusta (A.D. 29)

followed by the fall of Agrippina and her children.

There was another whom the Emperor had long looked at with unfriendly eyes. Asinius Gallus, a marked figure in the higher circles, had taken to his house the wife whom Tiberius had been forced indeed to put away, yet loved too well to feel kindly to the man who took his place. He had been named by the last Emperor among the few who might aspire to the throne, and was possibly the child the promise of whose manhood had been heralded by the fourth Eclogue of Virgil. He was certainly forward and outspoken, with something of presumption even in his flattery; he had often given offence by hasty words, and above all in the early scene of mutual mistrust and fear in the Senate House he had tried to force Tiberius to use plain language and drop his hypocritic trifling. He was made to pay a hard penalty for his boldness. The Emperor stayed his hand for years, allowed him to pay his court and join in the debates among the rest, and even summoned him to Capreæ to his table. But even while he sat there the news came that the Senate had condemned him at the bidding of their master, and he left the palace for a prison. For years he pined in utter loneliness, while the death which he would have welcomed as a boon was still denied him.

The fate of Asinius Gallus.

Meantime Sejanus ruled at Rome with almost absolute power. His master's seemingly unbounded trust made soldiers, senators, informers vie with each other in submissive service; his favor was the passport to preferment; his enmity was followed by a charge of treason or a threatening missive from Capreæ to the Senate. All classes streamed to his ante-chambers with their greetings, and the world of Rome flattered, feared or hated him. The Emperor heard all intelligence through him, colored and garbled

The great power of Sejanus at Rome.

as he pleased, approved his counsels, re-echoed his suspicions, and daily resigned more of the burden of rule into his hands. There had been no sign of mistrust even when he had asked for the hand of Livilla, the widow of the murdered Drusus, though consent had been delayed and reproof of his ambition hinted. Yet, wary as Sejanus was, he could not hide from envious eyes the pride and ambition of his heart. He grew haughtier with the confidence of power, and men whispered that in moments of self-indulgence he spoke of himself as the real autocrat of Rome, and sneered at his master as the Monarch of the Isle. But that master's eyes at length were opened. His brother's widow, Antonia, long retired from public life, had kept a watchful eye on all that passed, and sent a trusty messenger at length to warn him. He saw his danger instantly, felt it with a vividness that seemed to paralyze his will and stay his hand. For many months we have the curious picture of the monarch of the Roman world brooding, scheming, and conspiring against his servant. For months his letters were so worded as to keep Sejanus balanced between fear and hope. Sometimes he writes as if his health was failing, and the throne would soon be vacant, sometimes promotes his friend and loads him with caresses, and then again his strength is suddenly restored and he writes fretfully and sternly. The Senate is kept also in suspense, but notes that he no more calls the favorite his colleague, and that he raises a personal enemy to be consul. The bolt falls at last. Suddenly there arrives in Rome a certain Macro with letters from Capreæ for the Senate. He carries the commission in his pocket which

His haughtiness.

Suspicions of Tiberius at length aroused.

His dissimulation.

The scene in the senate-house.

makes him the new præfect of the guard, and had been told to concert measures with Laco, the præfect of the watch. He meets Sejanus by the way, alarmed to find that there is no message for himself, and reassures him with the tale that the letter brings him the high dignity of tribunician power. While Sejanus hurries in triumph to the Senate House, Macro shows his commission to the prætorians and sends them to their quarters far away, while Laco guards the Senate House with his watch. The reading of the Emperor's letter then begins. It is long and curiously involved in style, deals with many subjects, with here and there a slighting word against Sejanus, to which, however, he pays scant attention, as his thoughts are occupied with the signs of favor soon to follow. Suddenly comes the unlooked-for close. Two of his nearest intimates are denounced for punishment, and he is to be lodged at once in prison. Those who sat near had slipped away from him meantime; Laco with his guards is by his side, while the Senate rises on all sides and vents in angry cries the accumulated hate of years. He is dragged off to his dungeon. The people on the way greet him with savage jeers, throw down the statues raised long since in his honor, and the prætorians in their distant quarter make no sign. The Senate takes courage to give the order for his death, and soon all that is left of him is a name in history to point the moral of an unworthy favorite's rise and fall. His death rid Tiberius of his fears, but was fatal to the party who had looked to Sejanus as their chief, and possibly had joined him in treasonable plots against his master. Post after post brought the death-warrants of fresh victims.

where the Emperor's letter "verbosa et grandis epistola" is read,

and Sejanus is dragged off to death. A. D. 31.

Cruelty of Tiberius to the friends or partisans of Sejanus,

His kinsmen were the first to suffer, then came the turn of friends and tools. All who owed to him their advancement, all who had shown him special honor, paid the hard penalty of their imprudence. The thirst for blood grew fiercer daily, for the wife of Sejanus on her death-bed told the story of the poison of which Drusus died, and the truth was known at last. Tiberius had hidden his grief when his son died, and treated with mocking irony the citizens of Ilium who came somewhat late with words of condolence, telling them that he was sorry that they too had lost a great man named Hector; but the grief he had then not shown turned now to thirst for vengeance. On any plea that anger or suspicion could dictate fresh names were added to the list of the accused, till the crowded prisons could hold no more. The prætorians whose loyalty had been mistrusted were allowed to show how little they had cared for their commander by taking wild vengeance on his partisans; the populace also roamed the streets in riotous mobs to prove their tardy hatred for his memory In a passage of the Emperor's memoirs that has come down to us we read the charge that the fallen minister had plotted against Agrippina and her children. We may compare with this the fact that the order for the death of the second son was given after the traitor's fall. He was starved to death in the dungeon of the palace, after trying in his agony to gnaw the bed on which he lay, and the note-book of his gaoler gave a detailed account of his last words and dying struggles.

who now heard the cause of Drusus' death.

At Capreæ also there was no lack of horrors. There too the victims came to be tried under his eye, it is said to be even tortured, and to glut his thirst for bloodshed. He watched their agonies upon the rack, and was so busy with that

The trials and bloodshed at Capreæ,

work that when an old friend came from Rhodes at his own wish, he mistook the name of his invited guest and ordered him too to be tortured like the rest. Some asked to be put out of their misery by speedy death, but he refused, saying that he had not yet forgiven them. Even in trifling matters the like severity broke out. A poor fisherman climbed the steep rocks at Capreæ to offer him a fine lobster; but the Emperor, startled in his walk by his unbidden visitor, had his face gashed with its sharp claws to teach him more respect for rank. Nor is it only cruelty that stains his name. Sensuality without disguise or limit, unnatural lusts too foul to be described, debauchery that shrank from no excess, these are the charges of the ancient writers that brand him with eternal infamy. Over these it may be well to drop the veil and hasten onward to the close.

and foul debauches.

At length it was seen that his strength was breaking up, and the eyes of the little court at Capreæ turned to Caius, the youngest son of Agrippina and Germanicus, whom, though with few signs of love, he had pointed out as his successor. The physician whispered that his life was ebbing, and he sank into a swoon that seemed the sleep of death. All turned to the living from the dead and saluted him as the new Emperor, when they were startled with the news that the closed eyes were opened and Tiberius was still alive. But then—so ran the tale all Rome believed—the præfect Macro bade the young prince be bold and prompt: together they flung a pillow on the old man's head and smothered him like a mad dog as he lay.

His death, A.D. 37, hastened possibly by the hand of the young Caius.

The startling story of his later years is given with like features in the pages of three authors, Tacitus, Suetonius, and Dion Cassius, and none besides of ancient times describe his life or paint his character with any fulness of detail. But modern critics have come forward to contest the verdict of past history, and to demand a new hearing of the case. We must stay, therefore, to see what is the nature of their plea.

The pleas of the later critics in favor of a new estimate of the character of Tiberius.

They remind us that, at the worst, it was only the society of Rome that felt the weight of his heavy hand. Elsewhere, they say, through all the provinces of the vast empire his rule was wise and wary. His firm hand curbed the license of his agents; he kept his legions posted on the frontiers, but had no wish for further conquests, and in dealing with neighboring powers relied on policy rather than force. The shelter that he offered to the fugitive chiefs of Germany and the pretenders to the Eastern thrones gave them always an excuse for diplomacy and intrigues, which distracted the forces that were dangerous. Provincial writers like Strabo the geographer, Philo the philosopher, and Josephus the historian, speak of his rule with thankfulness and fervor; and the praises seem well-founded till we come to the last years of his life. Then, says Suetonius, he sunk into a sloth which neglected every public duty. He would not sign commissions, nor change the governors once appointed, nor fill up the vacancies that death had caused, nor give orders to chastise the neighboring tribes that disturbed the border countries with their forays. It is true the Empire was so little centralized as yet, and so much free life remained in the old institutions of the provinces, that distant peoples scarcely suffered from the torpor of the central

At the worst they say, Rome only suffered, while the Empire was well governed;

and this may be true, though with some qualification.

power, and, once relieved from the abuses of the old Republic, were well content if they were only left alone. Still the degradation of Rome, if real, must have reacted on them, for she attracted to the centre the notabilities of every land. She sent forth in turn her thought, her culture, and her social influence, and the pulsations of her moral life were felt in countries far away. The heroism of her greatest men raised the tone of the world's thought, and examples of craven fear and meanness surely tended to dispirit and degrade it.

Yet the degradation of Rome must have reacted on the world.

If we return now to the details of his rule at home what evidence can his defenders find to stay our judgment? They can point to the contemporary praises of Valerius Maximus, a literary courtier of the meanest type, and to the enthusiastic words in which Velleius Paterculus speaks of his old general's virtues. But the terms of the latter do not sound like a frank soldier's language; the style is forced and subtle, and the value of his praises of Tiberius may well be questioned when in the same pages we find a fulsome flattery of Augustus and Sejanus that passes all bounds of belief. We may note also that his history ends before the latter period of this reign begins. In default of testimony of a stronger kind, attention has been drawn to the marks of bias and exaggeration in the story commonly received, to the wild rumors wantonly spread against a monarch who had never won his people's love, and lightly credited by writers who reflected the prejudices of noble coteries offended by the unyielding firmness of his rule. On such evidence it has been thought enough to assume that the memoirs of Agrippina, Nero's mother,

The testimony of Valerius Maximus and Velleius Paterculus is not worth much.

The marks of bias and exaggeration in the common story.

The assumptions as to the memoirs of Agrippina, and the struggle between rival factions at Rome,

blackened the name of Tiberius and had a sinister influence on later history; to imagine a duel of life and death between the imperial government and the partisans of the widow and children of Germanicus; to believe, but without proof, that the chief victims of the times were all conspirators, who paid the just forfeit of their lives; to point to the malignant power of Sejanus and to fancy that the real clemency of Tiberius took at last a sombre hue in the presence of universal treachery. Whence this strange mania of disloyalty can have come is not made clear, nor how it was that of the twenty trusted senators chosen for the privy council only two or three were left alive, nor why Drusus, the son of Germanicus, was murdered when the fall of Sejanus had removed the tempter.

and the guilt of the victims of Tiberius, are made without any evidence.

Nor can the stories of the debauchery at Capreæ be lightly set aside without disproof. They left a track too lurid on the popular imagination, they stamped their impress even in vile words on the language of the times, and gave a fatal impulse to the tendencies of the corrupted art that left the records of its shame among the ruins of Pompeii.

Nor can we set aside the stories of the debauchery at Capreæ.

It may seem strange, indeed, as has been urged, that a character unstained for many years by gross defects should reveal so late in life such darker features. But we have no evidence which will enable us to rewrite the story of these later years, though on some points we have reason to mistrust the fairness of the historians whose accounts alone have reached us. They do seem to have judged too harshly acts

Ancient writers may have formed too harsh an opinion of his motives in some cases, and words which admit a fair and honorable color. Their conclusions do not always tally with the facts which they bring forward, and seem sometimes inconsistent with each other; the number and details of the criminal trials which they describe often fail to justify their charges of excessive cruelty in the emperor, and many of their statements as to his secret feelings and designs must have been incapable of proof. It was probably from prudence and not from mere irresolution that the prince continued his provincial governors so long in office; it may have been from true policy rather than from jealousy that he recalled Germanicus from useless forays on the border lands, from good sense rather than from want of spirit that he discouraged all excessive honors to himself. In these and many like cases Tacitus and other writers may have given a false reading of his motives, as they have certainly reported without weighing the scandalous gossip that blackened the memory of a ruler who discredited his best qualities by ungracious manners, and often made his virtues seem as odious as his vices.

and reported scandalous gossips too lightly;

But of the natural character of his younger years we know little. We see him trained in a school of rigid repression and hypocrisy, cowering under the gibes and censures of Augustus, wavering between the extremes of hope and fear, tortured by anxiety at Rhodes, drilled afterwards into an impassive self-restraint, till natural gaiety and frankness disappeared. When power came at last it found him soured by rancor and resentment, haunted by suspicion and mistrust, afraid of the Senate and Germanicus, and yet ashamed to own his fears; too keen-eyed to relish

but we know little of his earlier character, as he was trained in a school of rigid self-restraint and dissimulation.

flattery, yet dreading any show of independence; curbed by his mother, and spurred on by Sejanus into ferocity, inspired by fear; with an intellectual preference for good government, but still with no tenderness or sympathy for those whom he ruled. Possibly the partisans of Agrippina troubled his peace with their bold words and seditious acts, or even conspired to set her children in his place, and drove him to stern measures in his own defence. At length, when the only man whom he had fondly trusted played him false, his old mistrust settled into a general contempt for other men and for the restraints of their opinion. These safeguards gone, he may perhaps have plunged into the depths of cruelty and lust and self-contempt which made Pliny speak of him as the gloomiest of men—"tristissimus hominum,"—and led him to confess in his letters to the Senate that he was suffering from a long agony of despairing wretchedness. Even from the distant East we read, came the scornful letters in which the King of Parthia poured reproaches on the cruelty and debaucheries of his brother Emperor of the West.

CHAPTER III.

CALIGULA.—A.D. 37-41.

The general joy at the death of Tiberius

THE tidings of the gloomy emperor's death were heard at Rome with universal joy. The senators and men of mark began to breathe more freely after the reign of terror; the people who had suffered less, but for whom little had been done in the way of shows and largess, began to cry about the streets, "Tiberius to the Tiber!" and to talk of flinging his dishonored body like carrion to the crows.

All eyes turned with joy to the young Caius. The fond regrets with which they thought of Germanicus, his father, the memory of Agrippina's cruel fate, and the piteous stories of her murdered children, caused an outburst of general sympathy for the last surviving son. In early childhood he had been the soldiers' darling. Carried as a baby to the camp upon the Rhine, he had been dressed in mimic uniform and called by the familiar name of Caligula, from the tiny boots he wore like the legionaries around him. The mutinous troops who were deaf to the general's appeal were shamed into submission when they saw their little nursling carried for safety from their camp. For some years little had been known of him. After Agrippina's fall he had been brought up in seclusion by his grandmother Antonia, and thence summoned to Capreæ by the old Emperor while still a youth. He showed at that time a marked power of self-restraint, betrayed no resentments or regrets, and baffled the spies who were set to report his words. Yet Tiberius, who watched him narrowly, is said to have discerned the latent passions that were to break out one day in the license of absolute power; but still he advanced him to the rank of the pontificate, allowed him to be thought his probable successor, and named him in his will as co-heir with the young Tiberius, his grandchild. Besides this the præfect Macro was secretly won over to secure the support of the prætorian troops, and together they waited for and perhaps hastened the death of the old man. No

and at the accession of Caius,

named Caligula by the legionaries,

who had been at Capreæ with Tiberius,

and was named in his will as co-heir with the young grandchild, such support, indeed, seemed needed, for at Rome there was a popular movement in his favor. The people rushed into the Senate House with acclamations when he came, they showered endearing names upon him, the claims of his young cousin were ignored, and at the age of twenty-four Caligula became the sole monarch of the Roman world. The young sovereign was welcomed with a general outburst of excitement. Not only in the city which for long years had not seen its ruler, but even in the provinces, there were signs everywhere of wide-spread joy. In three months more than one hundred and sixty thousand victims fell in thanksgiving upon the altars. The young sovereign could scarcely be unmoved amid the general gladness. Senate, soldiers, people, all were lavish in their honors; the treasury was full of the hoards that had been gathering there for years; there was nothing yet to cross his will or cloud his joy. His first acts were in unison with the glad tone of public feeling, and did much to increase it. The exiles were brought back from the lonely islands where they pined; the works of the bold writers, Labienus and the like, were allowed once more to pass from hand to hand; the ardor of the informers cooled, and a deaf ear was turned to warning letters; the independence of the magistrates was re-asserted, and the accounts of the imperial budget fully published. Some show was even made awhile of restoring the elections to the popular vote, while a round of civic spectacles was arranged upon a scale of long disused magnificence.

whose claims, however, were ignored.

The general gladness,

return of the exiles,

and signs of brighter times.

The bright hopes thus raised were all shortlived. The extravagant popularity which had greeted him at first, the dizzy sense of undisputed power, were enough to turn a stronger head. His nervous system had always been weak. Epileptic from his boyhood, he suffered also from constant sleeplessness, and even when he slept his rest was broken with wild dreams. His health gave way soon after his accession; and the anxiety on all sides was so intense, the prayers offered for his recovery so excessive, that they seemed to have finally disturbed the balance of his reason. Henceforth his life is one strange medley of grandiose aims and incoherent fancies, relieved at times by lucid intervals of acute and mocking insight, but rendered horrible by a fiend's cruelty and a satyr's lust. In a short time Rome was startled by the news that its young Emperor claimed to be a god already. It was not enough for him to wait to be canonized like others after death. He towered already above the kings of the earth; the one thing wanting was to enjoy divine honors while he lived. To this end temples must rise at once to do him honor; priesthoods be established for his service; countless statues of the gods be brought from Greece and take in exchange the likeness of his head for their own. The palace was extended to the Forum, and the valley spanned with stately arches, that the shrine of Castor and Pollux might serve as a sort of vestibule to his own house, and that he might take his seat as by right between the heavenly brothers and be the object of admiring worship.

The Emperor's popularity and sense of power turned his head.

He claimed divine honors.

From a god something more is looked for than the works of man, and so he was always dreaming of great schemes. He threw a bridge across from Baiæ to Puteoli, upwards of three miles in length, and marched along it in state to furnish a two days' wonder to the world. He thought of building a city

Planned great schemes.

upon the highest Alps; with greater wisdom he wished to cut a channel through the Corinthian isthmus, and sent even to take the measurements needed for the work.

The heathen poets have often sung of the envy and jealousy of heaven; and the Emperor for a like cause could brook no rival. His young cousin Tiberius must die to expiate the crime of being once put upon a level with him; his father-in-law, Silanus, and his grandmother, Antonia, paid the forfeit of their lives for having formed too low an estimate of his majesty. Indeed, any eminence might be dangerous near him. Bald himself, he could not pass a fine head of hair without the wish and sometimes too the order that it should be shaved quite bare. He prided himself upon his eloquence, and two men nearly suffered for the reputation of their style. The first was Seneca, then much in vogue, who was saved only by a friend's suggestion that he was too far gone in a decline to live. The other, Domitius Afer, was a brilliant orator and notable informer. In vain had he foreseen his danger and tried to disarm jealousy by flattering words. He set up a statue to the Emperor to note the fact that he was consul a second time at the age of twenty-seven; but this was taken ill, as a reflection on the monarch's youth and unconstitutional procedure. Caius, who prided himself on his fine style, came one day to the Senate with a long speech ready-prepared against him. Afer was too wary to reply, but falling to the ground as if thunderstruck at eloquence so marvellous, only culled from memory the choicest passages of what he heard with comments on their beauties, saying that he feared the orator more than the master of the legions. The Emperor, delighted at praises from so good a judge,

Could bear no rival greatness,

as in the case of Seneca,

and Domitius Afer.

looked on him henceforth with favor. His spleen was moved not only by living worth but even by the glory of the dead. He threw down the statues of the famous men that graced the Campus Martius. He thought of sweeping from the public libraries the works of Virgil and Livy, but contented himself with harshly criticising them. The titles even that called up the memory of illustrious deeds provoked his umbrage; the old families must put aside the surnames of the Republic, and the Pompeian race drop the dangerous epithet of "Great."

Was jealous even of the dead.

The gods, it seemed, were above moral laws, for the old fables told of their amours without disguise or shame. Caius would be like Jupiter in this; indulge at once each roving fancy and change his wives from day to day. Invited at one time to a noble Roman's marriage feast, he stopped the rite and himself claimed the bride, boasting that he acted like Augustus and the Romulus of old time. His lewdness spared no rank nor ties of blood, but of all he loved Cæsonia best, who was famous only for her wantonness. He dressed her like an Amazon and made her ride to the reviews; and when she bore a child he recognised it for his own by the ferocity with which the infant seemed to scratch and claw everything she saw.

Thought himself raised above moral laws,

The oracles of old, from which men tried to learn the will of heaven, were couched often in dark mysterious terms, and in this spirit he delighted to perplex and to alarm. He summoned the senators from their beds at the dead of night, frightened them with strange sounds about them in the palace, then sung to them awhile and let them go. When the people clamored for a legal tariff of the new tolls and dues, he had one written out, but in characters

affected mystery, like the ancient oracles,

so small and so high-posted that no eyes could read it. His caprices often took a darker color. He heard that when he was once sick rash men had vowed to give their lives or face the gladiators if he grew better, and with grim humor he obliged them to prove their loyalty, even to the death.

and indulged in wild caprices.

We may see by the description of an eye-witness how great was the terror caused by these fitful moods of ferocity and folly. At Alexandria the Emperor's claims to deity had been regarded as impious by the Jews, but readily acquiesced in by the Greeks, who caught eagerly at any plea to persecute their hated rivals, and wreak the grudge of a long-standing feud. The synagogues were profaned with statues, the Jewish homes were pillaged without mercy, and complaints of disloyalty forwarded to Rome. The sufferers on their side sent an embassy to plead their cause, and at its head the learned Philo, who has left us an account to tell us how they fared. They were not received in state, in the presence of grave counsellors, but after long delay the two deputations of the Alexandrians and Jews were allowed to wait upon the Emperor while he was looking at some country houses near the bay of Naples. The Jews came bowing to the ground before him, but despaired when they saw the look of sarcasm on his face, and were accosted with the words, "So you are the impious wretches who will not have me for a god, but worship one whose name you dare not mention," and to their horror he pronounced the awful name. Their enemies, overjoyed at this rebuff, showed their glee with words and looks of insult, and their spokesman charged the Jews with wanton indifference to the Emperor's health and safety. "Not so, Lord Caius," they protested loudly, "for thrice we have sacrificed whole hecatombs in thy behalf."

"Maybe," was the reply, "but ye sacrificed for me, and not to me." This second speech completed their dismay, and left them all aghast with fear. But almost as he spoke, he scampered off, and went hurrying through the house, prying all about the room upstairs and down, cavilling at what he saw, and giving orders on his way, while the poor Jews had to follow in his train from place to place, amid the mockery and ribald jests of those about them. At length, after some direction given, he turned and said in the same breath to them, "Why do you not eat pork?" They tried to answer calmly that national customs often varied: some people, for example, would not touch the flesh of lambs. "Quite right, too," he said, "for it is poor tasteless stuff." Then the insults and the gibes went on again. Presently he asked a question about their claims to civil status, but cut them short in the long answer which they gave him, and set off at a run into the central hall, to have some blinds of transparent stone drawn up against the sun. He came back in a quieter mood, and asked what they had to say, but without waiting for the answer hurried off again to look at some paintings in a room close by. "At last," says Philo, "God in his mercy to us softened his hard heart, and he let us go alive, saying as he sent us off, 'After all they are to be pitied more than blamed, poor fools, who cannot believe I am a god.'"

His devices to refill his exhausted coffers.

His devices to refill the treasury, which his extravagance had emptied, showed no lack of original resource, though his plans were not quite after the rules of financial science. He put up to auction all the heirlooms of the past that had been stored in the imperial household, took an active part even in the sale, pointed out the rare old pieces with all the relish of a connoisseur, and gave the family pedigree of each. He made his courtiers push the prices up; and when one of them was sleepy he took each motion of the nodding head for a higher bid, and had a few gladiators knocked down to him at the cost of millions. When the news came of his daughter's birth he publicly bemoaned the costly burdens of paternity, and asked his loyal subjects for their doles to help him rear and portion the princess. He stood even at the entrance of his house on New Year's Day to receive with his own hands the presents showered on him by the crowd as they came to court. Oftentimes he did not stay to devise such far-fetched measures, but simply marked down wealthy men for confiscation, betook himself as far as Gaul in quest of plunder, and filled his coffers at the expense of the provincials. Even without such poor excuse he showed meantime a cruelty that seemed like the mere wantonness of a distempered fancy, as when he invited men to see him open a new bridge in state, and had the machinery contrived to fling crowds into the water; or when he laughed as he sat between the consuls and told them that a single word from him would make their heads roll off their necks; or when, to give his guests more zest for what they ate, he had the executioner ushered in to do his work before their eyes.

Resorted to confiscation.

Morbid ferocity.

One fiercer taste he seemed to lack—the love of war. But, suddenly reminded that recruits were wanted to make up the ranks of his Batavian body-guard, he took a fancy to a campaign in Germany, perhaps in memory of his father's name. Preparations were made on a grand scale, and he started for the seat of war, hurrying sometimes in such hot haste that his guards could scarcely keep be-

The campaign in Germany.

side him, and then again, lolling in lordly ease, called out the people from the country towns to sweep and water all the roads. As soon as he had reached the camp he made a great parade of the discipline of earlier days, degraded general officers who were late in coming with their troops, and dismissed centurions from the service on trifling grounds or none at all. Little came of all this show. A princely refugee from Britain asked for shelter. The Rhine was crossed, a parody of a night attack was acted out, and imposing letters were sent to the Senate to describe the submission of the Britons and the terror of the Germans. Then he hurried with his legions to the ocean, with all the pomp and circumstance of war, while none could guess the meaning of the march. At last when they could go no further he bade the soldiers pick up the shells that lay upon the shore and carry home their trophies as if to show in strange burlesque the vanity of schemes of conquest. Before he left the camp, however, the wild fancy seized him to avenge the insult offered to his majesty in childhood, and he resolved to decimate the legions that had mutinied long years before. He had them even drawn up in close order and unarmed before him, but they suspected danger and confronted him so boldly that he feared to give the word and slunk away to Rome. On his return he seemed ashamed to celebrate the triumph for which he had made costly preparations, forbade the Senate to vote him any honors, but complained of them bitterly when they obeyed.

Ludicrous close.

Still his morbid fancy could not rest, and wild projects flitted through his brain. He would degrade Rome from her place among the cities and make Alexandria, or even his birth-place, Antium, the capital of the world. But first he medita-

His wild dreams of massacre.

ted a crowning exploit to usher in the change with fitting pomp. It was nothing less than the massacre of all the citizens of mark. He kept two note-books, which he called his "sword" and "dagger," and in them were the names of all the senators and knights whom he doomed to death. But the cup was full already, and his time was come, though he had only had three years of power to abuse. He had often outraged with mocking and foul words the patience of Cassius Chœrea, a tribune of the guard. At last Chœrea could bear no more, and after sounding other officers of rank, who had been suspected of conspiracy already, and who knew their lives to be in danger, he resolved to strike at once. They took the Emperor unawares in a narrow passage at the theatre, thrust him through and through with hasty blows, and left him pierced with thirty wounds upon the floor.

CHAPTER IV.

CLAUDIUS.—A. D. 41–54.

FEW credited at first the tidings of the death of Caius; many thought the story was only spread by him in some mad freak to test their feelings, and so they feared to show either joy or grief. When at last they found it was true, and that Cæsonia and his child were also murdered, they noted in their gossip that all the Cæsars who bore the name of Caius had died a violent death, and then they waited quietly to see what the Senate and the soldiers thought of doing. The Senate met at once in the Capitol, where

The hesitation of the Senate after the murder of Caius

the consuls summoned to their guard the cohorts of the watch. There, with the memorials of the past, the tokens of ancient freedom, round them, they could take counsel with becoming calmness and dignity. The Emperor was dead, and there seemed no claimant with a title to the throne. Should they venture to elect a sovereign, regardless of the warnings of the past, or should they set up a commonwealth once more, and breathe fresh life into the shadowy forms about them? The discussion lasted all that day, and the night passed without a final vote. But it was all idle talk, for the prætorians meanwhile had made their choice. The tidings of the Emperor's death soon reached the camp, and drew the soldiers to the city. Too late to defend or even to avenge their sovereign, they dispersed in quest of booty, and roamed through the palace at their will. One of the plunderers passing by the alcove of a room espied the feet of some one hidden behind the half-closed curtains. Curious to see who it might be, he dragged him out, and recognized the face of Claudius, the late Emperor's uncle. He showed him to his comrades who were near, and, possibly in jest, they saluted him as their new prince, raised him at once upon their shoulders, and carried him in triumph to the camp. The citizens who saw him carried by marked his piteous look of terror, and thought the poor wretch was carried to his doom. The Senate heard that he was in the camp, but only sent to bid him take his place among them, and heard seemingly without concern that he was there detained by force. But the next day found them in different mood. The populace had been clamoring to have a monarch, the prætorians had sworn obedience to their new found emperor, the city

lasted till nightfall.

But the soldiers meantime had found Claudius,

carried him to the camp,

and saluted him Emperor.

guards had slipped away, and the Senate, divided and disheartened, had no course left them but submission.

Tiberius Claudius Nero Germanicus, the son of Drusus, grandson of Livia Augusta, suffered in early years from lingering diseases which left him weak both in body and in mind. The Romans commonly had little tenderness for sickly children. Antonia and his mother even spoke of him as a monster, as a thing which nature had rough-hewn but never finished; while his grandmother would not deign to speak to him except by messenger or letter. Though brought up in the palace he was little cared for, was left to the tender mercies of a muleteer, of whose rough usage he spoke bitterly in after life, and even when he came to manhood was not allowed to show himself in public life or hope for any of the offices of State. We may still read the letters written by Augustus to his wife, in which he speaks of him as too imbecile for any public functions, too awkward and ungainly to take a prominent place even in the circus at the show. The only honor which he gave him was a place in the priesthood of the augurs, and at his death he left him a very paltry legacy. Nor did Tiberius think more highly of him. He gave him only the poor grace of consular ornaments; and when he asked to have the consulship itself his uncle took no further notice than to send him a few gold pieces to buy good cheer with in the holidays. His nephew Caius made him consul, but encouraged the rough jests with which his courtiers bantered him. If he came late among the guests at dinner they shifted their seats and shouldered him away till he was tired of looking for an empty place; if

In early life he had been weak in mind and body, and had been despised or neglected.

He had sorry treatment from Tiberius

and Caius,

he fell asleep, as was his wont, they plastered up his mouth with olives, or put shoes upon his hands, that he might rub his eyes with them when he woke. He was sent by the Senate into Germany to congratulate the Emperor on his supposed successes; but Caius took it ill, and thought the choice of him was such a slight that he had the deputation flung into the river. Ever after he was the very last to be asked in the Senate for his vote, and when he was allowed to be one of the new priests the office was saddled with such heavy fees that his household goods had to be put up to auction to defray them. After such treatment from his kinsmen it was no wonder that he sank into coarse and vulgar ways, indulged his natural liking for low company, ate largely and drank hardly, and turned to dice for his amusement. Yet he had also tastes of a much higher order, kept Greeks of literary culture round him, studied hard and with real interest, and at the advice of the historian Livy took to writing history himself. His first choice of subject was ambitious, for he tried to deal with the troubled times that followed Julius Cæsar's death; but he was soon warned to leave so dangerous a theme. He wrote also largely on the history of Etruria and Carthage, and later authors often used the materials collected by or for him. Of the latter of the two works we read that a courtly club was formed at Alexandria to read it regularly through aloud from year to year.

and indulged in coarse habits;

but he had also literary tastes,

and took to writing history.

Such was the man who in his fiftieth year was raised to the Empire by a soldier's freak, to rule in name but to be in fact the puppet of his wives and freedmen. These were the real governors of the world, and their intrigues and rival-

As Emperor he was ruled by his wives and freedmen.

ries and lust and greed have left their hateful stamp upon his reign.

The freedmen had for a long time played an important part in the domestic life of Rome; for the household slaves that were so numerous at this time in every family of ample means could look commonly for freedom after some years of faithful service, though their old master still had legal claims upon them, and custom and old associations bound them to their patron and his children. They haunted the houses of the wealthy, filled all the offices of trust, and ministered to their business and pleasures. Among them there were many men of refinement and high culture, natives of Greece and Asia, at least as well educated as their masters, and useful to them in a hundred ways as stewards, secretaries, physicians, poets, confidants and friends. The Emperor's household was organized like that of any noble. Here, too, there were slaves for menial work, and freedmen for the posts of trust. The imperial position was too new and ill-defined, the temper of the people too republican as yet for men of high social rank and dignity to be in personal attendance in the palace; offices like those of high steward, chamberlain, great seal, and treasurer to the monarch had the stigma of slavery still branded on them, and were not such as noblemen could covet. But these were already posts of high importance, and much of the business of state was already in the freedmen's hands. For by the side of the Senate and the old curule officers of the Republic, the Empire had set up, both in the city and the provinces, a new system of administrative machinery, of which the Emperor was the centre and mainspring. To issue instructions, check accounts, receive reports, and keep the

The domestic position of the freedmen of Rome,

and in the imperial household.

needful registers became a daily increasing labor, and many skilful servants soon were needed to be in constant attendance in the palace. The funeral inscriptions of the time show that the official titles in the imperial household were becoming rapidly more numerous as the functions were more and more subdivided. When the ruler was strong and self-contained, his servants took their proper places as *valets-de-chambre*, ushers, and clerks, while a privileged few were confidential agents and advisers. When he was inexperienced or weak, they took the reins out of his hands, and shamefully abused their power. Much too low in rank to have a political career before them, they were not weighted with the responsibilities of power, and could not act like the cabinet ministers of modern Europe. The theory of the constitution quite ignored them, and they were only creatures of the Emperor, who was not the fountain of honor, like later kings, and could not make them noble if he would.

Important offices filled by them.

As high ambitions were denied them, and they could not openly assert their talents, they fell back commonly on lower aims and meaner arts. They lied and intrigued and flattered to push their way to higher place; they used their power to gratify a greedy avarice or sensual lust. Wealth was their first and chief desire, and their master's confidence once gained, riches flowed in upon them from all sides. To get easy access to the sovereign's ear was a privilege which all were glad to buy. The suitors who came to ask a favor, a post of profit or of honor; the litigants who feared for the goodness of their cause and wished to have a friend at court; vassal princes eager to stand well in the Emperor's graces, town councillors longing for some special

Their sordid ambition and greed,

and numerous opportunities

boon or for relief from costly burdens; provincials of every class and country ready to buy at any cost the substantial gift of Roman franchise. Hundreds such as these all sought the favorite in the antechamber, and schemed and trafficked for his help. There was no time to be lost, indeed, for a monarch's favor is an unstable thing, and shrewd adventurers like themselves were ever plotting to displace them. At any moment they might be disgraced, so they grasped every chance that brought them gain and speedily amassed colossal fortunes. Men told a story at the time with glee that when Claudius complained of scanty means a bystander remarked that he would soon be rich enough if two of his favorite freedmen would admit him into partnership.

of gaining wealth.

Now for the first time the personal attendants take a prominent place in public thought, and history is forced to note their names and chronicle their doings, and the story of their influence passes from the scandalous gossip of the palace to the pages of the gravest writers. In the days of his obscurity they had shared the meaner fortunes of their master, enlivened his dullness by their wit, and catered for his literary tastes. They had provided theories of style and learning and research, though they could not give him sense to use them, and now they were doubtless eager to help their patron to make history, not to write it. Greedily they followed him to the palace, and swooped upon the Empire as their prey.

Pallas.

Two of his old companions towered above all the rest, Pallas and Narcissus. The former had been with Claudius from childhood, and filled the place of keeper of the privy purse, or steward of the imperial accounts. In such a post, with such a master, it was easy for him to enrich himself, and he did not neglect his opportunities. But his pride was even more notable than his wealth. He would not deign to speak even to his slaves, but gave them his commands by gestures, or if that was not enough by written orders. His arrogance did not even spare the nobles and the Senate, but they well deserved such treatment by their servile meanness. The younger Pliny tells us some years afterwards how it moved his spleen to find in the official documents that the Senate had passed a vote of thanks to Pallas and a large money grant, and that he had declined the gift and said he would be content with modest poverty, if only he could be still of dutiful service to his lord. A modest poverty of many millions !

Narcissus.

Narcissus was the Emperor's secretary, and as such familiar alike with state secrets and with his masters' personal concerns. He was always at his side, to jog his memory and guide his judgment; in the Senate, at the law courts, in cabinet council, at the festive board, nothing could be done without his knowledge; in most events of moment his influence may be traced. Men chafed, no doubt, at the presumption of the upstart, and told with malicious glee of the retort made by the freedman of the conspirator Camillus, who, when examined in the council-chamber by Narcissus and asked what he would have done himself if his master had risen to the throne, answered, "I should have known my place, and held my tongue behind his chair." They heard with pleasure too that when he went on a mission to the mutinous soldiery in Britain, and tried to harangue them from their general's tribune, they would not even listen to him but drowned his voice with the songs of the Saturnalia, the festive time at Rome, when the slaves kept holiday and took their master's places. But at Rome none dared to be so bold, though his influence at court stirred the jealousy of many, who whispered to each other that it was no wonder he grew rich so fast when he made so much by peculation out of the great works which he prompted Claudius to undertake, and one of which at least, the outlet for the Lucrine Lake, caused almost a public scandal by its failure.

After them came Polybius, whose literary skill had often served his patron in good stead and gave him constant access to his ear. No sinister motives can be traced to him; at worst we hear that he was vain, and thought himself on a level with the best, and liked to take the air with a consul at each side. He had cool impudence enough, we read; for in the theatre, when the people pointed at him as they heard a line about a "beggar on horseback" who was hard to brook, he quoted at once another line from the same poet of the "kings that had arisen from a low estate."

Polybius.

Callistus lent to the new comers in the palace his long experience of the habits of a court. He had served under the last ruler, could suit his ways to please his new master so unlike the old, and soon took a high place among the ruling clique by his tact and knowledge of the world of Rome. Felix, too, whom we read of in the story of St. Paul, gained, possibly through his brother Pallas, the post of governor of Judea, but must have had rare qualities to marry, as Suetonius tells us, three queens in succession. Posides was the soldier of the party. His military powers, shown in the sixteen days' campaign of Claudius in Britain, raised him above other generals in his master's eyes, like his stately buildings which Juvenal mentions as out-topping the Capitol. There is no need to carry on the list.

Callistus.

Felix.

Posides.

These are only the most favored of the party, the best endowed with natural gifts, the most trusted confidants of Cæsar.

The first care of the new government was to reassure the public mind. Chœrea and his accomplices must die, indeed; for the murder of an Emperor was a fatal thing to overlook, and they were said to have threatened the life of Claudius himself. For all besides there was a general amnesty. Marked deference was shown by the new ruler to the Senate, and the bold words latterly spoken by its members were unnoticed. Few honors were accepted in his own name, while the statues of Caius were withdrawn from public places, his acts expunged from all official registers, and his claims to divine honors ignored, as those of Tiberius had been before. The people were kept in good humor by the public shows and merry-makings, as the soldiers had been by the promise of fifteen hundred sesterces a man; and so the new reign began amid signs of general contentment.

The new government tried to calm the public mind,

and to conciliate all classes.

The next care of the little clique was to keep their master in good humor, to flatter his vanities and gratify his tastes, while they played upon his weakness and governed in his name. This they did for years with rare success, thanks to their intimate knowledge of his character and to the harmony that prevailed among themselves. He had all the coarse Roman's love for public games, and was never weary of seeing gladiators fight; so they helped him to indulge his tastes and make merry with the populace of Rome. As the common round of spectacles was not enough, new shows must be lavishly provided. From the early

Claudius kept in good humor by his freedmen;

amused with spectacles

morning till the entertainment closed he was always in his seat, eager to see the cages of the wild beasts opened and to lose nothing of the bloody sport. The spectators could always see him, with his wagging head and the broad grin upon his slobbering mouth, could hear him often crack his poor jokes on what went on, sometimes noted with amusement how he hurried with his staggering legs across the arena to coax or force the reluctant gladiators to resume their deadly work. They noted also that he had the statue of Augustus first veiled and then removed from the scene of bloodshed, as if the cruel sport that amused the living must offend the saintly dead.

and good cheer.

He was fond also of good cheer, so fond of it that he sometimes lost sight of his dignity. One day as he sat upon the judgment-seat he smelt the savor of a burnt-offering in a temple close at hand, and breaking up the court in haste, he hurried to take his seat at dinner with the priests. At another time, in the Senate, when the discussion turned on licensing the public-houses, he gravely spoke about the merits of the different wine-shops where he had been treated in old days. So feasting was the order of the day; great banquets followed one upon the other, and hundreds of guests were bidden to his table, at which few ate or drank so freely or so coarsely as himself.

His love for judicial work,

But he had more royal tastes than these, for he aspired to be a sort of Solomon upon the seat of justice. As magistrate or as assessor by the curule chair, or in the Senate, when grave cases were debated, he would sit for hours listening to the pleaders or examining the witnesses, sometimes showing equity and insight, sometimes so frivolous and childish in his comments, that litigants and lawyers lost their patience altogether.

As the father of the people, it seemed one of his first cares to find his children bread, and no little time and thought were spent by him or by his agents in seeing that the granaries were filled and the markets well supplied. Yet the poor were not always grateful, for once when prices rose they crowded in upon him in the Forum and pelted him with hard words and crusts of bread, till he was glad to slink out by a back door to his palace. For his was certainly the familiarity that breeds contempt; his presence, speech, and character were too ungainly and undignified to impose respect; and even in his proclamations his advisers let him air his folly to the world. Sometimes he spoke in them about his personal foibles; confessed that he had a hasty temper, but that it soon passed away; and said that in years gone by he had acted like a simpleton to disarm the jealousy of Caius. Then again he put out public edicts as full of household cures and recipes as the talk of any village gossip.

and care for provisioning Rome

not always appreciated, by the people.

Want of dignity in his proclamations.

He had little taste for military exploits; yet once it was thought prudent to excite his martial ardor, that he might have the pleasure of a real triumph, like the commanders of old days. At the crisis of a campaign in Britain, when the preparations had been made for victory, the general sent to summon Claudius to the seat of war. All had been done to make the journey pleasant, the carriage even had been specially arranged to make it easy for him to while away the time by the games of dice which he loved so well; and though the waves and winds were not so complaisant or so regardful of his comforts, he reached at last the distant island, in time to

A campaign and victory arranged for him.

receive the submission of the native princes and to be hailed as Emperor on the battle-field.

Meanwhile the freedmen reaped their golden harvest; having early agreed upon a common course of action, they divided the spoil without dispute. They trafficked in the offices of state, bestowed commissions in the army, sold the verdicts of the law courts, and put up the Emperor's favor to the highest bidder. One privilege, which millions craved, the citizenship of Rome, was above all a source of income to the favored freedmen, who could get their master's signature to any deed. He has, indeed, in history the credit of a liberal policy of incorporation, and speeches are put into his mouth in which he argues from the best precedents of earlier days in favor of opening the doors to alien races. It may be that his study of the past had taught him something; but it is likely that the interest of his ministers did more to further a course which in their hands was so lucrative a form of jobbery. It was a common jest to say that the market was so overstocked at last that the franchise went for a mere song.

Scandalous traffic of the freedmen,

especially in the grant of citizenship,

which may account for his liberality in that respect.

But these, after all, were petty gains, and they needed a more royal road to wealth. They found it in a new kind of proscription. They marked out for death and confiscation those who had houses or gardens which they coveted, made out the rich men to be malcontents and the city to be full of traitors. It was easy to work upon the Emperor's fears, for he had always been an abject craven, and was always fancying hidden daggers. A telling story, a mysterious warning, or a dream invented for the purpose, almost anything

They confiscate the property of the rich by working on their master's fears, could throw him off his balance and make him give the fatal order. Nor did they always wait for that. One day a centurion came to give in his report. He had, in pursuance of his orders, killed a man of consular rank. Claudius had never known of it before, but approved the act when he heard the soldiers praised for being so ready to avenge their lord. When the list was made out in later times, it was believed that thirty-five members of the Senate and some three hundred knights fell as victims to the caprice or greed of the clique that governed in the name of Claudius, many of them without any forms of justice, or at best with the hurried mockery of a trial in the palace. So fatal to a people may be the weakness of its rulers. It was noticed as a scandalous proof of his recklessness in bloodshed that he soon forgot even what had passed, and bade the very men to supper whose death-warrant he had signed, and wondered why they were so late in coming.

who soon forgot that he had given the fatal order.

The guilt of these atrocities must be shared also by his wives. Of these Claudius married several in succession, but two especially stand out in history for the horror of all times.

His wives.

Messalina's name has passed into a byword for unbounded wantonness without disguise or shame. Her fatal influence ruined or degraded all she touched. The pictures painted of her in old writers give no redeeming features in her character, no single unselfish aim or mental grace, nothing but sensual appetites in a form of clay. Her beauty gained her an easy command over her husband's heart, but not content with that her wanton fancy ranged through every social order and shrank from no impure advances Some whom she

Messalina.

Her unbounded wantonness

tempted had repelled her in their virtue or disgust, but her slighted love soon turned to hatred, and on one false plea or other she took the forfeit of their lives. For she had no scruples or compunction, no shrinking from the sight of blood; and pity, if she ever felt it, was with her only a mere passing thrill, a counter-irritant to other feelings of the flesh. The Roman Jezebel coveted, we read, the splendid gardens of Lucullus, and to get them had a lying charge of treason brought against Valerius Asiaticus, their owner. His defence was so pathetic as to move all those who heard him in the Emperor's chamber, and to make even Messalina weep. But as she hurried out to dry her tears she whispered to her agent, who stood beside, that for all this the accused must not escape.

and cruelty.

For a long time she was wise enough to court or humor the confederates of the palace, and so far her course of crime was easy. At last she threw off such restraints of prudence, turned upon Polybius, who had taken her favors in too serious a mood, and rid herself for ever of his ill-timed jealousy. The other freedmen took his fate as a warning of defiance to them all, looked for a struggle of life and death, and watched their opportunity to strike. The chance soon came, for Messalina cast her lustful eyes on a young noble, and did not scruple to parade her insolent contempt for Claudius by forcing Silius to public marriage. It was the talk of the whole town, but the Emperor was the last to know it. Then Narcissus saw the time was come, and, though the rest wavered, he was firm. In concert with his confidants he opened the husband's eyes, and worked skilfully upon his fears with dark warnings

At last she defied the freedmen

by killing Polybius,

and causes public scandal by marrying Silius.

about plots and revolution; prevented any intercourse between them, lest her wiles and beauty might prove fatal to his scheme, and at last boldly ordered her death, while Claudius gave no sign and asked no question. She died in the gardens of Lucullus, purchased so lately by the murder of their owner.

Narcissus tells Claudius,

and procures her death.

The Emperor soon after made a speech to his guards upon the subject, bemoaned his sorry luck in marriage, and told them they might use their swords upon him if he ever took another wife. But his freedmen knew him better, and were already in debate upon the choice of a new wife. Callistus, Pallas, and Narcissus each had his separate scheme in view, and the rival claims broke up the old harmony between them. The choice of Pallas fell on Agrippina, the daughter of Germanicus and niece of Claudius. Married at the age of twelve to Cn. Domitius Ahenobarbus, a man of singular ferocity of temper, she had brought him a son who was to be one day famous. She had been foully treated by Caligula, her brother, and banished to an island till his death. Recalled by Claudius, she learnt prudence from the fate of the two Juliæ, sister and cousin, who fell victims to the jealousy of Messalina. She shunned all dangerous rivalry at court, and was content to exchange her widowhood for the quiet country life of a new husband, one of the richest men in Rome, who, dying shortly after, left Domitius his heir, and gave her back her freedom when the time was come for her to use it. Her first care was to gain a powerful ally at court. She found one soon in Pallas, who was as proud and ambitious as herself, and she stooped to be the mistress of a minion while aspiring to be an Emperor's wife.

Debate among the freedmen as to the choice of a new wife.

Agrippina, his niece, carries off the prize,

When Pallas pleaded for her in the council-chamber, where the merits of the different claimants were long and anxiously discussed, she did not spare to use her feminine wiles upon the weak old man. By right of kinship she had a ready access to the palace, and could lavish her caresses and her blandishments upon him. The fort besieged so hotly fell at once, and she was soon his wife in all but name. For a while he seemed to waver at the thought of shocking public sentiment by a marriage with his niece; but those scruples were soon swept aside by the courtly entreaties of the Senate and the clamor of a hired mob.

who showed at once her intention to rule supreme,

Agrippina showed at once that she meant to be regent as well as wife. She grasped with a firm hand the reins of power, still relied upon the veteran statecraft and experience of Pallas, and maintaining with him the old intrigue, broke up the league of the confederates. The feminine rivals whose influence she feared were swept aside by banishment or death. Lollia above all had crossed her path, and seemed likely to carry off the prize. She did not rest till the order was given for her death and a centurion despatched to bring her head. Then—so runs the horrid story—to make sure that the ghastly face was really that of the beautiful woman she had feared and hated, she pushed up the pallid lips to feel the teeth, whose form she knew. Then she felt that she was safe, and received the title of Augusta from the Senate. She had the doings of her court reported in the official journals of the day, and gave the law to all the social world of Rome. Two children of Claudius, by Messalina, Britannicus and Octavia, stood in the path of her ambition.

swept aside her rivals,

especially Lollia;

had Octavia betrothed to her son,

Of these the latter was at once betrothed to her young son, who was pushed forward rapidly in the career of honors, ennobled even with proconsular authority, and styled "Prince of the Youth" even in his seventeenth year. Meantime the star of the young Britannicus was paling, and men noted with suspicion that all the trusted guards and servants of the boy were one by one removed and their places filled with strangers. Of the freedmen of the palace Narcissus only had not bowed before her; with gloomy look and ill-concealed suspense he still watched over his patron and his children. His strength of character and long experience gave him a hold over his master that was still unshaken, and Agrippina did not dare to attack him face to face. But his enmity was not to be despised. He had sealed the doom of one wife—he might yet destroy another. There was something to alarm her also in the mood of Claudius, weak dotard as he was, for strange words fell from him in his drunken fits, coupled with maudlin tenderness for his own children and suspicious looks at Nero. There seemed no time, therefore, to be lost, and she decided to act promptly. She seized the opportunity when Narcissus was sent away awhile to take the waters for the gout; and while his watchful eye was off her, she called to her aid the skill of the poisoner Locusta and gave Claudius the fatal dose in the savory dish he loved.

and the trusted servants of Britannicus removed.

Afraid of Narcissus and of delay,

she had Claudius poisoned.

Scarcely was he dead when Seneca wrote for the amusement of the Roman circles a withering satire on the solemn act by which he was raised to the rank of the immortals. In a medley of homely prose and lofty verse he pictures the scene above at the moment of the Emperor's

The satire of Seneca on the deification of Claudius.

death. Mercury had taken pity on his lingering agony, and begged Clotho, one of the three Fates, to cut short his span of life. She tells him that she was only waiting till he had made an end of giving the full franchise to the world. Already by his grace Greeks and Gauls, Spaniards and Britons wore the toga, and only a few remnants were still left uncared for. But at length she lets loose the struggling soul. Then the scene shifts to heaven. Jupiter is told that a stranger had just come hobbling in, a bald old man, who wagged his head so much and spoke so thick that no one could make out his meaning, for it did not sound like Greek or Roman or any sort of civilized speech. Hercules, as being used to monsters, is deputed to ask him whence he comes, and he does this as a Greek in words of Homer. Claudius, glad to find scholars up in heaven who may perhaps think well of his own works of history, caps the quotation with another about a short journey made to Troy, and might have imposed on the simple-minded god, if the goddess Fever had not come up at that moment from the Roman shrine where she was worshipped, and said that he was only born at Lugdunum, in the country of the old Gauls, who, like himself, had taken the capital by storm. Claudius, in his anger, made the usual gesture by which he ordered men's heads off their shoulders, but no one minded him any more than if they had been his own proud freedmen; so, remembering that he could not strut and crow any more on his own dunghill, he begs Hercules to befriend him and to plead his cause in the council-chamber of the gods. This he does with some effect, and when the debate opens most of the speakers seem inclined to let Claudius come in. But at length Augustus rises, and with

The scene when Claudius arrives in heaven.

The debate as to his admission

energy denounces his successor, who had shed so much noble blood like water, and murdered so many of the family of the Cæsars without a trial or a hearing. His speech and vote decide the question, and Claudius is dragged away to Hades with a noose about his throat like the victims of his cruelty. As he passes on his way through Rome his funeral dirge is being sung, and he hears the snatches of it which mentioned in his praise that no one ever was so speedy on the seat of judgment, or could decide so easily after hearing one side only, or sometimes neither; and that pleaders and gamblers would keenly feel the loss of a monarch who had loved so much the law, court, and the dice-box. The spirits in Hades raise a shout of triumph when they hear that he is near, and all whom he had sent before him throng about him as he enters. There they stand, the intimates, the kinsmen he had doomed to death, the senators, the knights, and less honored names as countless as the sand on the seashore, and silently confront the fallen tyrant. But Claudius, seeing all the well-known faces, forgetting, as he often did in life, or even ignorant of the causes of their death, said, "Why, here are all friends! How ever came you hither?" Then they curse him to his face and drag him to the chair of Æacus, the judge, who condemns him unheard, to the surprise of all, save the criminal himself. After some thought a fitting penalty was found. Claudius was doomed to play for all eternity with a dice-box that had no bottom.

turns against him after the protest of Augustus.

He is dragged away to Hades;

and passing through Rome, hears the dirges on himself.

The spirits of his victims crowd in triumph round him,

and drag him before the judge, to receive his fitting doom.

CHAPTER V.

NERO.—A.D. 54–68.

We read that when Domitius was told that he had a son, he said that any child of his by Agrippina must prove an odious and baneful creature. The mother asked her brother Caius, the Emperor, to give the child a name, but he pointed to Claudius, his laughing-stock, and said that the little one should bear his name, though the mother angrily protested at the omen. Soon afterwards he lost his parent's care by death and banishment, and was brought up at the house of his aunt Lepida, entrusted to the charge of a dancing-master and a barber, till brighter times came back with the return of his mother from her place of exile. He rose with Agrippina's rise to power, and became the central object of her ambitious hopes; for, the sister of one emperor and wife of another, she was determined to be the mother of a third. At the age of ten she had him made the adopted son of Claudius, when he took the name of Nero. The choice of Seneca to be his tutor met with the approval of men of worth and culture; the appointment of Burrhus to be the sole præfect of the prætorian guard secured the support of the armed force of Rome. His betrothal to Octavia strengthened his claims still further, and stirred the jealousy of the young Britannicus and the grave fears of the old servants like Narcissus. The issue showed how well-founded were those fears. As soon as the death of Claudius was made

The early life of Nero.

Brought forward by his mother, and adopted by Claudius,

known, Nero, hurrying to the camp of his advisers, spoke the soldiers fairly, and making ample promises of largess, was saluted Emperor by acclamation. The claims of Britannicus were set aside, and no voice was raised even in the Senate in his favor.

he was saluted as Emperor by the soldiers.

At first the strong will of Agrippina seemed to give the tone to the new government. Votes were passed in her honor by the Senate; the watchword given to the soldiers was, "The best of mothers." To satisfy her resentment or to calm her fears Narcissus had to die. That she might take her part in all concerns of the State the Senate was called to the palace to debate, where behind a curtain she could hear and not be seen. But the two chief advisers of the prince, though they owed their places to her favor, had no mind to be the tools of a bold bad woman, behind whom they could still see the form of the haughty minion Pallas.

His mother Agrippina tried at first to govern,

The præfect of the prætorians, Afranius Burrhus, who wielded the armed force of the new government, was a man of grave and almost austere character, whose name had long stood high at Rome for soldierly discipline and honor. His merits had given him a claim to his high rank, and he would not stoop to courtier-like compliance. He used his weighty influence for good, though he had at times to stand by and witness evil which he was powerless to check.

but Burrhus, the præfect of the guard,

L. Annæus Seneca represented the moral force of the privy council, though he had the more yielding and compliant temper of the two. Sprung from a rich family of Corduba, in Spain, his wealth and good connections and brilliant

and Seneca, the former tutor of Nero,

powers of rhetoric had made him popular in early life with the highest circles of the capital, till he gained to his cost the favor of the Emperor's sister. Banished by the influence of Messalina, he had turned to philosophy for comfort, and won high repute among the serious world of Rome by the earnestness and fervor of his letters. Few stood higher among the moral writers of the day, no one seemed fitter by experience and natural tastes to be director of the conscience of the young nobility.

took the reins out of her hands,

With rare harmony, though different methods, the two advisers used their influence to sway the young Emperor's mind and to check the overweening pride of Agrippina. They took the reins of power from her hand and reassured the public mind, which had been unnerved by the despotic venal government of late years, with its tyrant menials and closest trials. They restored to the Senate some portion of its old authority and chose the public servants wisely. For five years the world was ruled with dignity and order, for the young Emperor reigned in name, but did not govern, and the acts that passed for his were grave and prudent, while the very words even were put into his mouth for state occasions. When the Senate sent a vote of thanks he bade them keep their gratitude till he deserved it; and when he had to sign a death-warrant, he said that he wished he was not scholar enough to write his name. The pretty phrases were repeated; men did not stay to ask if they were Seneca's or Nero's, but hoped that they might prove the key-note of the new reign. But the two ministers meantime had cause for grave misgivings, for they had long studied their young charge with watchful eyes, and had seen with regret how little they

and ruled in his name with dignity and prudence,

though they saw cause for grave misgivings.

could do to mould his character as they could wish. Burrhus had failed to teach him in the camp any of the virtues of a soldier; all the lessons of temperance, hardihood, and patience left no traces in his mind. Seneca had been warned, we read, by Agrippina that the quibbles of philosophy would be too mean for his young pupil. He had little taste himself for the orators of the Republic, and did not care to point to them for lessons of manly dignity and freedom. But he did his best to teach him wisdom, spoke to him earnestly of duty, wrote for him moral treatises, full of thought and epigram, on themes like clemency and anger, but could not drop the language of the court, and hinted in his very warnings that the prince was raised above the law—was almost a god to make and to destroy.

In spite of their effort to form his tastes

Nero even from his youth had turned of choice to other teachers. He had little taste for the old Roman drill in arms and law and oratory, and was, it was noted, the first of the emperors who had his speeches written for him, from lack of readiness in public business. But he had a real passion for the arts of Greece, for music, poetry, and acting; had the first masters of the age to train him, studied with them far into the night, and soon began to pride himself upon the inspiration of the Muses. To gain time for such pursuits he was well content to leave the business of State to graver heads, and to take his part only in the pageant. He had other pleasures of a meaner stamp. Soon it was the talk of Rome that the young Emperor stole out in disguise at night, went to low haunts or roved about the streets with noisy roysterers like himself, broke into taverns and assaulted quiet citizens, and showed

he showed a passion for the fine arts

and for low dissipation.

even in his mirth the signs of latent wantonness and cruelty.

His boon companions were not slow to foster the pride and insolence of rank, to bid him use the power he had, and free himself without delay from petticoat rule and the leading-strings of greybeards. Their counsels fell on willing ears. He had long been weary of his mother. She had ruled him as a boy by fear rather than by love, and now she could not stoop willingly to a lower place. She wanted to be regent still, and hoped perhaps to see her son content to sing and act and court the Muses, while she governed in his name. But he had listened gladly to ministers who schooled him to curb her ambition and assert himself. He looked on calmly while they checked her control over the Senate, put aside her chief adviser, Pallas, annulled the despotic acts of the last reign, and took the affairs of state out of her hands. She was not the woman to submit without a struggle. There were stormy scenes sometimes between them, and then again she tried with a woman's blandishments to recover the ground that she had lost. She talked of the wrongs of the young Britannicus, and spoke of stirring the legions in his favor. As Nero's love for Octavia cooled she took to her home the injured wife and made public parade of sympathy and pity. When it was too late, she changed her course of action, condoned and offered even to disguise the amorous license on which she had frowned before so sternly, and tried in vain to win his love with a studied tenderness that would refuse him nothing.

His impatience of his mother's restraint, encouraged by his advisers,

Nero's chief ministers had put him on his guard against her and roused his jealousy and fear. They had now to stand by and see the struggle take its course, and watch the outcome with a growing horror. Britannicus, of whose name such impudent use was made, was stricken at dinner with a sudden fit and taken out to die, as all men thought, by poison. His poor sister hid her grief in silence, but she was soon to be divorced Agrippina was first stripped of all her guard of honor and forced to leave her house upon the Palatine; false informers were let loose upon her and wanton insolence encouraged. It was murmured that the dread Locusta was at work brewing her poisonous drugs, and that three times they tried in vain to poison her. One day it was found that the canopy above her bed was so arranged that the ropes must soon give way, and the whole crush her as she lay in sleep. At length Nero could wait no longer, and he found a willing tool in Anicetus, the admiral of his fleet, and between them a dark plot was hatched. It was holiday-time, and Nero was taking the baths at Baiæ. Suddenly he wrote a letter to his mother full of sorrow at the past estrangement and of hopes that they might live on better terms if she would only come and see him as of old. She came at once, and found a hearty welcome; was pressed to stay on one plea or another till at last night was come. Nero conducted her to a barge of state and left her with tender words and fond embraces. She was not far upon her homeward way across the bay, when at a signal given, the deck fell crashing in and the barge rolled over on its side; and the crew, far from coming to the rescue, struck with their oars at Agrippina and her women as they struggled in the water. But she was quiet and kept afloat awhile, till a boat picked her up and carried her to her

was carried by him to lengths they had not dreamt of.

Treatment of Britannicus and Octavia.

The attempts to poison Agrippina failed.

The dark scheme to drown her in the Bay of Naples.

home, to brood over the infamous design. At last she sent a messenger to tell her son that she was safe though wounded. Nero, baffled in his murderous hopes and haunted by fears of vengeance, was for awhile irresolute. He even called into counsel Seneca and Burrhus, and told them of his plot and of its failure. They would have no hand in her death, though they had no hope, perhaps no wish to save her. While they talk Anicetus acts. He hastens with an officer or two to Agrippina's house, makes his way through the startled crowd about the shore, and finds her in her bed-room all alone. There, while she eyes them fiercely and bids them strike the womb that bore the monster, they shower their blows upon her and leave her lifeless body gashed with wounds.

Its failure,

followed by her murder. A. D. 59.

The ministers of Nero must share the infamy of this unnatural deed. They had already tarnished their good name by mean compliance. To save the power that was slipping from their grasp they had closed their eyes to Nero's vices: they had tried even to cloak his youthful passion for a freedwoman by a paltry subterfuge; they had held their peace when Britannicus was poisoned, and stooped even to share the bounties that were showered at the time upon the courtiers; and now they sunk so low in good men's eyes as to defend the deed from the thought of which even Nero at first shrunk aghast. Burrhus, we read, sent officers of the prætorian guard to announce the soldiers' joy that their sovereign was safe for ever from his mother's plots. Seneca's hand drew up the despatches to the Senate in which the murdered woman was charged with treasonable designs against the Emperor's life, and all the worst horrors of

Burrhus and Seneca, to their disgrace, defended the deed,

the days of Claudius were raked up to cover her memory with shame. The Senate, too, was worthy of its prince, and voted solemn thanksgivings for his safety, while Thrasea alone protested by his silence, and walked out of the house at last when he could brook their flattery no longer. Even distant cities found an excuse for mean servility. One deputation came to beg Nero in the name of the provincials to bear his heavy grief with patience.

and public opinion condoned it.

The Emperor came back to Rome to find the city decked out in festive guise to greet him like a conquering hero. So, rid at length of all fear of rivalry or moral restraints from his advisers, he gave free vent to his desires. Music and song, the circus and the theatre had been the passion of his childhood; they were now to be the chief object of his life. He shared the tastes of the populace of Rome, and catered for them with imperial grandeur. No cost or care was spared to make the spectacles imposing and worthy of the master of the world. The old national prejudice had looked on the actor's trade as almost infamous for freeborn Romans; but Nero drove upon the stage citizens of rank, knights and senators of ancient lineage, and made them play and act and dance before the people. The historian Dion Cassius rises from his sober prose almost to eloquence when he describes the descendants of the conquered races pointing the finger at the sons of the great families from which their victors sprung; the Greeks asking with surprise and scorn if that was indeed Mummius, the Spaniards marveling to see a Scipio, the Macedonians an Æmilius before them. At last, as if it were to cover their disgrace—or, as many thought, to share it—Nero appeared himself in public, and

Nero gave himself up to his pleasures,

drove free-born Romans on the stage,

and at last appeared on it himself,

sang and played and acted for the prize, and sought the plaudits of the crowd. He did not take it up as the mere pastime of an idle day, but practised and studied in real earnest, showed feverish jealousy of rival actors, and humbly bowed before the judges, as if the contest was a real one. No one might leave the theatre while he played; Vespasian was seen to nod, and sunk at once in his good graces. Five thousand sturdy youths were trained to sit in companies among the audience and give the signal for applause. Not content with such display at Rome, he starred it even in the provinces. The Greeks were the great connoisseurs of all the fine arts; in their towns were glorious prizes to be won, and Greece alone was worthy of his voice and talents. Greece was worthy also of her ruler; nowhere was adulation more refined, nowhere did men flatter with more subtle tact the pride and vanity of the artist-prince.

taking to it in real earnest.

We cannot doubt that Nero had a genuine love of art. It may seem as if he lived to justify the modern fancy that art has a sphere and canons of its own, and may be quite divorced from moral laws. But indeed the art of Nero and his times was bad, and that because it was not moral. It set at naught the eternal laws of truth and simplicity, of temperance and order. In poetry and music it was full of conceits and affectations, straining after the fantastic. In plastic art size was thought of more than beauty of proportion, and men aimed at the vast and grandiose in enormous theatres and colossal statues. In place of the delicate refinement of Greek taste its drama sought for coarse material effects; it did not try by flight of fancy to stir the nobler feelings of the heart, but relied

Nero had a real love of art:

but the art was bad, because it was immoral.

on sensuous pageantry and carnal horrors to goad and sate the morbid taste for what was coarse, ferocious, and obscene.

Nero's life as Emperor was one long series of stage effects, of which the leading feature was a feverish extravagance. His return from the art-tour in Greece outdid all the triumphal processions of the past. Thousands of carriages were needed for his baggage; his sumpter mules were shod with silver; and all the towns he passed upon his way received him through a breach made in their walls, for such he heard was the "sign of honor" with which their citizens were wont to welcome the Olympian victors of old days. The public works which he designed were more to feed his pride than serve the public. He wanted, like another Xerxes, to cut a canal through the Corinthian isthmus; thought of making vast lakes to be supplied from the hot springs of Baiæ, and schemed great works by which the sea might be brought almost to the walls of Rome. But it was only by his buildings that he left enduring traces, and to this the great disaster of his times gave an unlooked-for impulse. Some little shops in the low grounds near the Circus took fire by chance. The flames spread fast through the narrow streets and crowded alleys of the quarter, and soon began to climb up the higher ground to the statelier houses of the wealthy. Almost a week the fire was burning, and of the fourteen wards of the city only four escaped unharmed. Nero was at Antium when the startling news arrived, and he reached Rome too late to save his palace. He threw his gardens open to the homeless poor, lowered at once the price of corn, and had booths raised in haste to shelter them.

Nero's extravagant display,

especially in building,

to which the great fire of Rome gave fresh impetus.
A.D. 64.

He did not lack sympathy for the masses of the city, whose tastes he shared and catered for. And yet the story spread that the horrors of the blazing city caught his excited fancy, that he saw in it a scene worthy of an Emperor to act in, and sung the story of the fall of Troy among the crashing ruins and the fury of the flames. Even wilder fancies spread among the people: men whispered that his servants had been seen with lighted torches in their hands as they were hurrying to and fro to spread the fire. For Nero had been heard to wish that the old Rome of crooked streets and crowded lanes might be now swept clean away, that he might rebuild it on a scale of royal grandeur. Certainly he claimed for himself the lion's share of the space that the flames had cleared.

The strange rumors as to his conduct,

and suspicions.

The palace to which the Palatine hill had given a name now took a wider range and spread to the Esquiline, including in its vast circuit long lines of porticoes, lakes, woods, and parks; while the buildings were so lavishly adorned with every art as to deserve the name of the "Golden House" which the people's fancy gave to them. In its vestibule stood the colossal figure of the Emperor, one hundred and twenty feet in height, which afterwards gave its name to the Colosseum. From it stretched porticoes a mile in length, supported on triple ranges of marble pillars, leading to the lake, round which was built a mimic town, opening out into parks stocked with wild animals of every sort. The halls were lined with gold and precious stones; the banqueting-rooms were fitted with revolving roofs of ivory, perforated to scatter flowers and perfumes on the guests, while shifting tables seemed to vanish of themselves and

He had the "Golden House" built for him on the most splendid scale, re-appear charged with richest viands. There were baths too to suit all tastes, some supplied from the waters of the sea, and some filled with sulphurous streams that had their sources miles away.

Thousands of the choicest works of art of Greece and Asia had been destroyed, but their place was taken by the paintings and the statues brought from every quarter of the empire. Nero sent special agents to ransack the cities for art-treasures, and many a town among the isles of Greece mourned in after days the visit that had despoiled it of some priceless treasure.

and furnished with the art-treasures of Greece.

When all was done and the Emperor surveyed the work, even he was satisfied, and he cried, " Now at least I feel that I am lodged as a man should be." It was in halls like these that the privileged few gathered round their lord when he returned from the grave business of the circus and the stage to indulge in the pleasures of the table. Otho, the profligate dandy, who had been complaisant enough to lend his wife to Nero; Tigellinus, præfect of the guards, ready to pander to his master's worst caprices; Vatinius, the hunchback, who had left his cobbler's bench and pushed his fortunes in the palace by his scurrilous jests and reckless attacks on honest men; Sporus, the poor eunuch, and Pythagoras, the freedman, both degraded by the mockery of marriage with the wanton prince—these and many another whose names have not been gibbeted in history left their memories of infamy in that " House of Gold."

Its most privileged inmates.

The mood of the citizens meanwhile was dark and lowering as they brooded over their disasters, and Nero looked to find some victims to fill their thoughts or turn their suspicion

To turn suspicion from himself,

from himself. The Christians were the scapegoats chosen.

Nero made the Christians his victims and his scapegoats,

Confused in the popular fancy with the Jews, whose bigotry and turbulence had made them hated, looked upon askance by Roman rulers as members of secret clubs and possible conspirators, disliked probably by those who knew them best for their unsocial habits or their tirades against the fashions of the times, the Christians were sacrificed alike to policy and hatred. They deserved their fate, says Tacitus, not, indeed, because they were guilty of the fire, but from their hatred of mankind. There was a refinement of cruelty in their doom. Some were covered with the skins of beasts, and fierce dogs were let loose to worry them. Others were tied to stakes and smeared with tar, and then at nightfall, one after another, they were set on fire, that their burning bodies might light up Nero's gardens, while the crowds made merry with good cheer, and the Emperor looked curiously on as at the play. No wonder that in the pages even of the heathen writers we hear something like a cry of horror, and that in the Christian literature we may trace the lurid colors of such scenes in the figures of Antichrist and in the visions of the coming judgment.

with a refinement of cruelty in torturing them.

But Nero did not often waste his thought and ingenuity on such poor prey as the artizans and freedmen of the Christian Churches. His victims were commonly of higher rank, and the nearer to him the nearer they seemed to death. His aunt followed his mother to the grave, and her tender words to him as she lay upon her death-bed were rewarded by a message to her doctor to be prompt and close her pains. Octavia was soon divorced and killed, on a

But his victims were commonly of higher rank.

His aunt,

His wife, Octavia,

charge of faithlessness, which was so carelessly contrived as to shock men by its very wantonness of power. Poppæa, her successor, was dearly loved, and yet he killed her in a fit of passion with a hasty kick. He soon wearied of the grave face of Burrhus, who read in his coolness the omen of a speedy death. Before long he grew sick and felt that he was poisoned. He pointed to the blood that he spat up as the signs of princely gratitude, would not see Nero when he called to ask him how he felt, but said only, "Well," and turned his face away and died. Seneca was longer spared, but he too felt that his time must come. He held himself aloof from court, tried to give up all his wealth and honors, to live austerely, and by the lessons of philosophy to make himself strong and self-contained, or to be director of the consciences of those who needed help and comfort.

Poppæa,

Burrhus,

Seneca spared for a time.

But with a prince like Nero even students were not safe, and philosophy itself was dangerous ground. The noblest minds at Rome were at this time mainly Stoics, and among the long line of Nero's victims there were many who were in some sense martyrs to the Stoic creed. They were not republicans, though they have sometimes passed for such in later history. They were not disloyal, though they were looked at with disfavor. They were ready to serve the ruling powers either in the Senate or the camp; there was a largeness even in their social views as citizens of the world that would seem to fit them markedly for carrying out the levelling spirit of the imperial policy. Nevertheless they were regarded with jealousy and mistrust; nor is the reason far to seek. Stoicism in passing from the schools of Greece had ceased

Philosophers were looked on with mistrust.

Stoicism,

to be an abstract theory, with interest only for the curious mind that loved the subtleties of paradox. It was a standard of duty for the Romans, and a creed to live and die for. The resolute spirit and the hard outlines of its doctrines had a fascination for the higher type of Roman mind. To live up to the ideal of a noble life, in which reason should rule and virtue be its own reward; to care very much for a good conscience, for personal dignity and freedom, and to think slightingly of short-lived goods over which the will has no control —here was a rule that was not without a certain grandeur, however wanting it might be at times in tenderness and sympathy. But such high teaching was distasteful to the sensualist and tyrant; its tone rebuked his follies and his vices. It set up a higher standard than the will of Cæsar, and was too marked a contrast to the servile flattery of the times. It was not the spiritual Quixotism of a few, which might be safely disregarded, but men flocked to it on every side for lessons of comfort and of hardihood in evil days. Weak women turned to it to give them strength, as Arria, in the days of Claudius, had shown her husband how to die, when she handed him the dagger that had pierced her with the words, "See, Pætus, it does not hurt." Some spread the doctrines with a sort of apostolic fervor, and may well have said at times uncourtly things of the vices in high places, like the Puritan preachers of our own land. Some again, mistook bluntness of speech for love of truth, like Cornutus, who, when some one pressed Nero to write a work in some four hundred books, remarked that "no one then would read them; it was true Crysippus wrote as many, but they were of some use to mankind." Others, influencing the world of fashion in quiet inter-

especially distasteful to the prince,

but spread rapidly through society.

course and friendly letters, showed the young how to live in times of danger; or when the fatal message came stood by and calmed the pains of death, like the father-confessors of the Church.

The character and fate of Thrasea Pætus.

Of the great Stoics of that time there was no more commanding figure than that of Thrasea Pætus. He had none of the hard austerity of a Cato nor the one-sided vehemence of a social reformer; he was fond even of the play, and mixed gaily in the social circles of the city; would not blame even vice severely, for fear of losing sight of charity to men. In the Senate he was discreet and calm, even when he disliked what was done; tempered his blame with words of praise, spoke of Nero as an eminent prince, and voted commonly with his colleagues, though he did not stoop to mean compliance. Sometimes, indeed, he protested by his silence, as when he rose and left the Senate-house rather than hear the apology of Nero for the murder of his mother, and when he declined to come and join the vote for the apotheosis of Poppæa. At last, when the evils seemed too strong for cure, he would take no part in public actions. For the last three years of his life he would not sit in his place among the senators, nor take the yearly vow of loyalty, nor offer prayer or sacrifice for Cæsar. The rebuke of his silence was a marked one, for the world, watching his bearing, turned even to the official journals to see what Thrasea had not done, and to put their construction on his absence. The calm dignity of his demeanor seems to have awed even Nero for a while, but at last the Emperor wearied of his quiet protest. The fatal order found him in his garden, surrounded by a circle of his kinsmen and choice spirits, with whom he tranquilly conversed upon high themes. Like another Socrates he heard his doom with cheerfulness, and passed away without a bitter word.

Seneca, too, found consolation but not safety in the Stoic doctrines. He had long retired from the active world, and shunned the Emperor's jealous eye. He had sought in philosophy the lessons of a lofty self-denial, and was spending the last years of his life in studying how to die. The rash conspiracy of a few of his acquaintance, in which he took no part himself, was the excuse, though not the motive, for his murder. The sentence found him with his young wife and intimates, prepared for but not courting death. Denied the pleasure of leaving them by will the last tokens of affection, he told his friends that he could bequeath them only the pattern of an honest life, and gently reproved the weakness of their grief. His veins were opened; but he talked on still while life was slowly ebbing, and was calm through all the agony of lingering death.

Of Seneca, (A. D. 65),

Corbulo, the greatest soldier of his day, whose character was cast in an antique mould, and was true to the traditions of the camp, had also to experience the ingratitude of princes. He had led his troops to victory in the North, had baffled the Parthian force and guile, and saved a Roman army from disaster; he had been so loyal to his Emperor in the face of strong temptation as to cause the Armenian Tiridates to say in irony to Nero that he was lucky in having such a docile slave. Suddenly he was recalled with flattering words. The death warrant met him on his way, and he fell upon his sword, saying only, "I deserved it." So unlooked for was the deed that men could only say that Nero was ashamed to meet his eye while busied in pursuits so unworthy of a monarch.

and of Corbulo. (A. D. 67).

A crowd of other victims pass before us on the scene. The least distinguished were driven forth from Rome to people lonely islands, while the chiefs proved to the world that they had learned from the Stoic creed the secret how to live nobly and die grandly. Women too were not wanting in heroic courage. Paulina, the young wife of Seneca, tried to go with him to the grave. Others were glad to save their self-respect by death. Of these some fell as victims to the jealousy of Cæsar; their eminence, their virtues, and historic names made them dangerous rivals. Some found their wealth a fatal burden when the Emperor's wild extravagance had drained his coffers and fresh funds were needed for his lavish outlay. More frequently they died to expiate a moral protest, which was often silent, but not the less expressive. The absolute ruler was provoked by men who would not crouch or bend. He felt instinctively that they abhorred him, and fancied that he saw even in the look of Thrasea something of the sour pedagogue's frown. Their fate marked the crisis of the struggle between high thought and ignoble acting.

Other victims, women among the number, suffered for different reasons.

Lucan too at this time, by a less honorable death, closed a short life of poetic fame. He had risen to early eminence in the social circles of the capital, stood high in favor at the court, where the passion for the fine arts was in vogue, and, as the nephew of Seneca, he shared the studies and for a time the confidence of Nero. But the sunshine of princely favor was soon clouded; he was coldly welcomed in the palace, and then forbidden to recite in public. What was the reason of the change we cannot say with certainty. Perhaps he was too bold

Lucan fell into disgrace at court,

in the choice of his great subject. The civil wars of the Republic had seemingly a fascination for the literary genius of this time, and many a pen was set to work and many a fancy fired by the story of the men who fought and died in the name of liberty or for the right to misgovern half the world. There was, of course, a danger in such themes. Julius Cæsar had written an Anti-Cato, to attack a popular ideal, and later rulers might be tempted to meet his eulogists with the sword rather than the pen. Historians had already suffered for their ill-timed praises of the great republicans; and Claudius had been warned not to meddle with so perilous a theme. Lucan, therefore, may well have given offence to the instinctive jealousy of a despot, though he was not sparing of his flattering words, as when he bids him take a central place among the heavenly constellations, for fear of disturbing the equilibrium of the world; and in the opening books, at least, which alone had seen the light, he was wary and cautious in his tone. Or it may be he offended Nero's canons of poetic style, for he cast aside the old tradition and boldly dispensed with the dreamland of fable and all the machinery of the marvellous and superhuman. He aspired to set history to heroic verse, but claimed no knowledge of the world unseen. Or, as it is more likely still, his fame gave umbrage to his master, who was himself a would-be poet, and could not bear to have a rival. Whatever may have been the cause of his disgrace, Lucan could not patiently submit to be thus silenced. His vanity needed the plaudits of the crowd; his genius perhaps seemed cramped and chilled for the want of kindly sympathy. For the habit of public readings, then so

from his choice of subject

or of style,

or excited the jealousy of Nero.

In his resentment

common, took to some extent the place of the journals and reviews of modern times, and brought an author into immediate relation with the cultivated world for whom he wrote. When this pleasure was denied him Lucan first distilled into his poem some of the bitterness of his wounded pride, and then joined a band of resolute men who were conspiring to strike down the monarch of whom they were long weary and to set up a noble Piso in his place. The plot came to an untimely end, and most of those who joined it lost their lives. Lucan lost not his life only, but his honor, for when his fears were worked upon he gave evidence against his friends, and even denounced his mother as an accomplice in the plot. We can have little pity when we read that he could not save his life even by such means, nor can we feel interest in the affected calmness with which, in his last moments, he recited from his poem an account of death-agonies somewhat like his own.

he took part in a conspiracy,

and lost both life and honor.

There died at the same time the chief professor of a very different creed from that of the great Stoics. Petronius had given a lifetime to the study of the refinements of luxurious ease: his wit and taste and ingenuity had made him the oracle of Roman fashion, or the "arbiter," as he was called, of elegance. Nothing new could pass current in the gay world of the city till it had the stamp of his approval. He was the probable author of a satire which curiously reflects the tone of social thought around him, its self-contempt, its mocking insight, and its shameless immorality. The work is a strange medley. It contains among other things a specimen of a heroic poem on the

Petronius Arbiter,

the probable author of a curious satiric novel,

same theme as that of Lucan's, full of the mythological machinery which the bolder poet had eschewed, and intended, therefore, possibly as a protest against Lucan's revolutionary canons. It gives us also, in the supper of Trimalchio, a curious picture of the tasteless extravagance and vulgar ostentation of the wealthy upstarts of the times, such as might please the fastidious pride of the nobles in Roman circles. It might amuse them also, sated as they were with fashionable gossip, to hear the common people talk, and to be led in fancy into the disreputable haunts through which the hero of the piece is made to wander in the course of strange adventures, like a "Gil Blas" of old romance. The writer, if he really was Petronius, roused at last a jealousy which caused his ruin; for the vile favorite, Tigellinus, who had gained the ear of Nero, and aspired to be the master of ceremonies at the palace, could not bear a rival near him. He trumped up a false charge against him, worked upon his master's fears which had been excited lately by the widespread conspiracy of Piso, and had an order sent to him to keep away from court. Petronius took the message for his death-warrant, and calmly prepared to meet his end. He set his house in order, gave instructions to reward some and punish others of his slaves, wrote out his will, and composed a stinging satire upon the Emperor's foul excesses which he sealed and sent to him before he died. It was noted that at last no philosopher stood at his bedside to whisper words of comfort or dwell on hopes of immortality, but that true, even in death, to his ignoble, godless creed, he amused himself as the streams of life were ebbing with frivolous epigrams and wanton verses.

excited the jealousy of Tigellinus as a leader of the fashions,

was banished from court,

and died with frivolous indifference.

Besides the portents of cruelty and lust, confined mainly to the walls of Rome, other disasters were not wanting to leave their gloomy traces on the annals of the times. A hasty rising of the British tribes under Queen Boadicea was followed by the sack of two great Roman colonies, Camalodunum and Londinium, and the loss of seventy thousand men. In Armenia a general's incapacity had brought dishonor on the legions and nearly caused the loss of Syria. Italy had been visited with hurricane and plague; and the volcanic forces that had been long pent up beneath Vesuvius gave some token of their power by rocking the ground on which Pompeii stood and laying almost all its buildings low.

The rising in Britain, and great loss of life,

and other great disasters of the time.

It was the monarch's turn at length to suffer some of the agony now felt around him; and after fourteen years he fell because the world seemed weary of him, and none raised a hand in his defence. The signal of revolt was given first in Gaul, where Vindex, a chieftain of a powerful clan of Aquitania, roused the slumbering discontent into a flame by describing, as an eye-witness, the infamy of Nero's rule and the ends to which the heavy taxes were applied. He told them of Sporus carried as a bride in Nero's litter, and submitting publicly to his caresses; of Tigellinus lording it at Rome, and making havoc among noble lives, while his master was fiddling in all the theatres of Greece; of Poppæa Sabina, first his mistress then his wife, who had her mules shod with shoes of gold, and five hundred asses daily milked to fill her bath; of the countless millions wrung from toiling subjects and squandered on a vile favorite or a passing fancy. Waiving all hopes of personal ambition, he urged Galba,

The revolt of Vindex, in Gaul,

the governor of Spain, to lead the movement, and came to terms with Verginius Rufus, who was marching from Germany against him. He killed himself, indeed, soon after with his own hand in despair, when the soldiers of Verginius fell upon his followers without orders from their general; but Galba was moving with his legions, and courier after courier arrived in Rome to say that the West of the Empire was in arms.

taken up by Galba after the death of Vindex.

Nero heard the tidings first at Naples, but took little heed of anything except the taunts of Vindex at his sorry acting; and even when he came at length to Rome he wavered between childish levity and ferocious threats. Sometimes he could think only of silly jests and scientific toys, sometimes he dreamed of fearful vengeance on the traitors and their partisans in Rome, and then again he would drop into maudlin lamentations, talk of moving his legions to sympathy by pathetic scenes, or of giving up the throne to live for art in humble peace. He tried to levy troops, but none answered to the call; the prætorian guards refused to march, the sentries even slunk away and left their posts, while the murmurs grew hourly more threatening, and ominous cries were heard even in the city. Afraid to stay within the palace, he went at night to ask his friends for shelter; but the doors of all were barred. He came back again to find his chambers plundered, and the box of poisons which he had hoarded gone. At length a freedman, Phaon, offered him a hiding-place outside the walls; and barefooted as he was, with covered face, Nero rode away to seek it. As he went by the quarters of the soldiers he

Nero's indifference at first,

followed by strange alternations of hope and despair.

Deserted on all sides,

he fled away at night to a freedman's house,

heard them curse him, and wish Galba joy. At last he and his guide leave the horses and creep through the brushwood and the rushes to the back of Phaon's house, where on hands and feet he crawls through a narrow hole which was broken through the wall. Stretched on a paltry mattress, in a dingy cell, hungry, but turning in disgust from the black bread, with the water from the marsh to slake his thirst, he listens with reluctance to friends who urge him to put an end to such ignoble scenes. He has a grave dug hastily to the measure of his body, and fragments of marble gathered for his monument, and he feels the dagger's edge, but has not nerve enough to use it. He asks some of the bystanders to show him by their example how to die, and then he feels ashamed of his own weakness and mutters, "Fie, Nero! now is the time to play the man." At last comes Phaon's courier with the news that the Senate had put a price upon his head; the tramp of the horses tells him that his pursuers are on his track, and fear gives him the nerve to put the dagger to his throat, while, true to the passion of his life, he mutters, "What a loss my death will be to art!" Stoicism had taught his victims how to die with grand composure; but all his high art and dramatic studies could not save him from the meanest exit from the stage. His last wish was granted, and they burnt the body where it lay, to save it from the outrage that might follow. Two poor women, who had nursed him as a baby, and Acte, the object of his boyish love, gathered up his ashes and laid them beside the rest of his own race.

and hid himself awhile in an agony of suspense,

then at last found nerve to kill himself.

It might be thought that few but his own pampered favorites could retain any affectionate remembrance of

Strange affection for his memory shown by some of the populace.

such a monster of sensuality and cruel caprice, who at his best was moody and volatile, undignified and vain; yet it seems that a fond memory of him lingered in the hearts of many of the people, who brought their flowers to deck his grave or posted up proclamations which announced that he was living still and would come to take vengeance on his enemies. Pretenders started up from time to time and gathered adherents round them in his name, and even after twenty years one such adventurer, of humble birth, received from the Parthians a welcome and support, and was reluctantly abandoned by them at the last.

Pretenders appeared in his name.

CHAPTER VI.

GALBA.—A.D. 68–69.

The career of Galba before his accession.

THE accession of Sulpicius Galba was due to a stir of independence in the provinces. Gaul would not brook the rule of Nero longer, and the chief who came forward in the name of Vindex to maintain their liberty of choice, and whose fiery proclamations hurled Nero from his throne, called upon Galba to succeed him. He came of ancient lineage, though unconnected with the family which through natural ties or by adoption had given six emperors to Rome. Early omens are said to have drawn upon him as a boy the notice of Augustus and Tiberius; he was hotly courted by the widowed Agrippina, and took a high place among the legatees of Livia Augusta in the will that was not carried out. Many years of his life were spent in high command in Africa, Germany, and Spain, where he became eminent for energy and strict discipline, bordering at times on harshness, till he put on a show of easy sloth to disarm the jealousy of Nero. The force at his command was small. A single legion and two troops of horse formed but a scanty army to carry an Emperor to Rome. His soldiers showed no great enthusiasm for him, and some of his cavalry were minded even to desert him. When he heard the news of the death of Vindex he despaired not of success only but of life, and thought of ending his career by his own hand.

As governor of Spain, he had only a small force, which was not hearty in his cause,

So far he had appealed only to the province that he ruled, had begun to levy troops and strengthen his tiny army, and to form a council of provincial notabilities to advise him like a senate. He called himself the servant only of the Roman State. But when the tidings came that the capital had accepted him for their new ruler he took at once the name of Cæsar, and put forth without disguise imperial claims. Rival pretenders started up at once around him. In Africa, in Germany, in the quarters of the Prætorian guards, generals came forward to dispute the prize, for every camp might have its claimant when the power of the sword would give a title to the throne; but one after another fell, while their soldiers wavered or deserted them. So Galba made his way to Rome without a struggle. But before him came the rumors of his harshness and his parsimony. He had sternly fined and punished the cities that were slow to recog-

but was accepted by the populace instead of Nero.

Rival pretenders rose and fell,

and Galba made his

way to Rome without a struggle, but preceded by ugly rumors,

nise him, and put men to death unheard as partisans of the fallen causes. Ugly stories reappeared of the severities of earlier days—of the money-changer whose hands he had nailed to the bench where he had given false weight, of the criminal for whom he had provided in mockery a higher cross than usual, as he protested that he was a citizen of Rome. There was little to attract the people in the sight of their new prince, who entered Rome upon a litter, with hands and feet crippled by the gout, and face somewhat cold and hard, marked already with the feebleness of old age.

and with no attractive look.

The soldiers were the first to murmur. The marines whom Nero had called out mutinied when they were sent back to join their ships, but they were sternly checked and decimated. The imperial body-guard of Germans was disbanded and sent back home empty-handed. The prætorians, ashamed already of the death of Nero and their præfect, heard with rage that the new sovereign would not court their favor or stoop to buy the loyalty of his soldiers. The legions on the frontier were ill-pleased to think that their voices counted for so little, that they were not thought worthy of a word or promise. The German army chafed because their general Verginius had been removed on flattering pretexts, but really because his influence over them was feared; and they construed his forced absence from the camp as an insult to their loyalty, and the exceptional favors shown to some towns of Gaul as a marked affront offered to themselves. Nor was the city populace in a cheerful mood. For years they had been feasted and ca-

Discontent of the marines, prætorians, legionaries and city populace.

ressed; races and games, gladiators and wild beasts had made life seem a holiday and kept them ever in good humor. Now they heard that there was to be an end to all such cheer, for their ruler was a morose, penurious old man, who thought a few silver pieces awarded to the finest actor of the day a present worthy of a prince.

Nero's servants and favorites,

Nero's favorites and servants heard with rage that they must disgorge at once the plunder of the past *regime*. A commission was appointed to call them to account and to wrest from them what their master's prodigality had given, and as a special grace to leave them each a beggarly tithe of all the presents, in which he had expended during the few years of his reign no less than two thousand one hundred millions sesterces. The Senate and the men of worth and rank were full of hope at first, for Galba seemed upright and spoke them fair. But soon they found, to their dismay, that all influence had passed out of their hands, and that the Emperor himself was not the ruling power in the State. Three favorites—one a freedman, Icelus; two of higher rank, T. Vinius, his legate, and Cornelius Laco, an assessor in his court of justice—had followed him from Spain, and gained, as it seemed, an absolute control over his acts. They never left him, and the wits of Rome called them the Emperor's pedagogues; indeed, they seemed to guide the old man as by the leading-strings of childhood, and to recall the memory of the worst days of the dotard Claudius. Public offices of trust, boons, immunities, and honors were put up shamelessly to auction, and the life and honor of free men were sacrificed to the caprice and greed of haughty and venal minions, while the most infamous of Nero's creatures,

and of the Senate.

The favorites of Galba shamelessly abuse their power.

Tigellinus, was saved by their influence from the fate he merited.

In a short time the discontent was universal. Already the legions of the Rhine had refused the oath of loyalty, and called on the Senate and the people to choose another Emperor, while in the city the temper of all classes boded ill. But Galba took one more step, and that was fatal. Feeling that at the age of seventy-three he had not strength to rule alone, he decided to adopt a colleague and successor. His choice fell on Piso Frugi Licinianus, who was young, noble, and of eminent worth. But the act came too late to regain the confidence that had been lost, and only provoked a speedier explosion of fear, jealousy, and disaffection; the more so because the speech in which he told the soldiers of his choice was of almost disdainful brevity, and irritated minds that were still wavering and might have been won over by a little timely liberality.

Galba adopted Piso as his colleague;

The blow came from the prætorian camp in which two common soldiers undertook to give away the throne, and kept their word. A freedman had tampered with them in the interest of his master Otho, who had hoped to take the place that Piso filled, and who would now try foul means, as fair had failed. The soldiers felt the temper of their comrades, and Otho's intimates and servants were lavish with their presents to the guard on all occasions. While Galba stood one morning beside the altar on which the victim lay, and the priest read presages of disaster in the entrails, Otho was beckoned suddenly away on the plea of buying an old property with the advice of his architects and builders. In the Forum he found twenty-three prætorians, who hurried him

but Otho intrigued with the soldiers of the guard,

was suddenly hurried off to

in a litter to their camp, and then presented him to the homage of their comrades. All were soon won over with fair words and liberal promises of bounty. The marines had not forgiven the Emperor his harsh treatment of their comrades, and therefore joined the movement eagerly, while the armed forces quartered in the city made common cause with the insurgents, thrusting aside the officers who tried to hold them in.

the camp, and saluted Emperor.

Rumors passed rapidly through Rome meanwhile. At first men heard that the guards were up in arms against their prince and had carried off a senator, some said Otho, to their camp. Messengers were dispatched at once by the startled rulers to secure if possible the obedience of the other forces, while Piso appealed to the company on guard around the palace to be staunch and true even though others wavered, and then set out to face the insurgents in the camp. Shortly after came the news that the prætorians had slain Otho to assert their loyalty, and that they were coming to salute their sovereign. The false news spread, designedly or not, and all classes who had hesitated before streamed into the palace to make a show of joy, and to conduct Galba to the camp, while one soldier in the crowd waved in the air his sword, dripping, as he said, with Otho's blood. But the Emperor, mindful of discipline to the last, said, "Comrade, who bade you do the deed?" At length he started, after much debate and doubt, but could make little way among the densely crowded streets, and hardly reached the Forum, when the insurgent troops appeared in sight. They were joined at once by his single company of guards; together they charged and dispersed the crowd

Alarming rumors spread rapidly through Rome,

and Galba after much hesitation, set out for the camp;

that followed him, while the slaves that bore the litter flung it down upon the ground and left their master stunned and helpless and undefended, to be hacked to death by the fierce soldiery that closed about him. So died, says Tacitus, one whom all would have thought fit for empire, had he not been Emperor in deed. There were many claimants for the honor of dispatching him, and Vitellius received more than one hundred and twenty letters of petition from men who looked for high reward for such a signal merit. To save the trouble of deciding and to discourage so dangerous a precedent, he ordered all the suitors to be put to death.

but while on his way was set upon and killed;

Piso had fled for sanctuary meantime to Vesta's temple, where a poor slave took pity on him and gave him the shelter of his hut. But the emissaries of Otho were soon upon the spot to drag him from his hiding-place and slay him on the temple steps and take his head to feast his master's eyes. The friends of the fallen rulers were allowed by special favor to buy their bodies from the soldiers, and show them the last tokens of respect.

and Piso, who had fled to sanctuary, was slain at the temple steps.

CHAPTER VII.

OTHO.—A. D. 69.

M. SALVIUS OTHO began in early youth a wild and dissolute career. To gain a footing in the palace he paid his court to an old waiting-maid of influence, and before long became one of the most prominent of the set of young roysterers who surrounded Nero. He rose to be the chief friend and

Otho's early career of dissipation.

confidant of the young prince, encouraged him in his worst excesses, was privy even to his mother's murder, and gave the luxurious supper which lulled her fears to rest. He relied too much, however, on his influence, and presumed to be the Emperor's rival for the heart of Poppæa Sabina, after giving her his hand and home to cloak Nero's wanton love. To cover his disgrace and check the scandalous gossip of the city he was appointed to official duties in Lusitania, where for ten years his equity and self-restraint were a marked contrast to the infamy of his earlier and later life. In Galba's rise to power he saw his opportunity of return, and he exhausted all his arts of flattery and address in the attempt to win the old man's favor, with the further hope that he might take the place which the Emperor's death would soon vacate. That hope once baffled, he calmly laid his plans, and swept away without compunction the obstacles that barred his road to power. On the evening of the day when Galba fell he made his way across the blood-stained Forum to the palace, while the Senate in a hurried meeting passed all the usual votes of honor for their new prince. The populace were ready with their cheers, and pressed him to take the name of Nero, in memory of the revels of his youth. But the real power was in the soldiers' hands, and they watched with jealous care the puppet they had set upon the throne. He had nothing of the soldier's bearing, was effeminate in look and carriage, with beardless face and an ungainly walk. Yet, strange to say, they loved him well, and were loyal to him to the last. They kept watch and ward with anxious care that no evil might befall him. They once flew to arms in ground-

Of better repute in provincial rule.

Returned to Rome with Galba,

and displaced him.

He gained the soldiers' loyalty and love.

less panic when he was seated with his friends at supper, forced their way even to his presence, to make sure that their favorite was safe; and when he died some slew themselves in their despair, as the dog dies upon his master's grave. Otho could refuse them nothing. He let them choose their own commanders, listened readily to all their grievances, gave them freely all they asked for, and had recourse to subterfuges to rescue from their clutches some whom he wished to spare. He had soon need of all their loyalty, for even before Galba's death the armies of the Rhine had hailed as Emperor their general Vitellius, and their legions were already on the march for Rome. For they were weary of the monotony of constant drill and border camps, and flushed with triumph at the ease with which they had crushed the hopes of Vindex. They cast greedy eyes on the wealth of Gaul, and were jealous of the privileged prætorians; they felt their power and longed to use it, now that the fatal secret had been learnt, that emperors were not made at Rome alone.

But the armies of the Rhine had chosen Vitellius as their Emperor,

So leaving Vitellius himself to follow slowly with the levies newly raised, two armies made their way to Italy, with Valens and Cæcina at their head, and crossing the Alps by different passes, after spreading terror among the peoples of Gaul and Helvetia, met at last upon the plains of Lombardy. Letters meantime had passed between Vitellius and Otho, in which each urged the other to abate his claims, and to take anything short of the imperial power. From promises they passed to threats, and thence to plots. Each sent assassins to destroy the other, and each failed to gain his end. But the legions of the North came daily nearer, and Otho lost no time in mustering

and were on the march for Rome.

his forces, and showed an energy of which few had thought him capable. He could count upon the army in the East, where Vespasian was acting in his name. The nearer legions in Pannonia and Dalmatia were true to him, and would soon be ready to join the forces that he led from Rome. So with such household troops as he could gather and the questionable contingent of two thousand gladiators, he set out to meet the enemy and to appeal to the decision of the sword. With him there went perforce many of the chief officers of state, the senators of consular rank, nobles and knights of high position : some proud of their gay arms and trappings, but raw and timid soldiers for the most part, thinking often more of the pleasures of the table than of the real business of war. But their presence in the camp gave moral support to Otho's cause, and lessened the danger of disaffection in the rear. His most skilful generals urged delay till his distant forces could come up from Illyria or the East; but his soldiers were rash and headstrong and, flushed by slight successes at first over Cæcina, accused their chiefs of treachery. His confidants were inexperienced and sanguine, and Otho would not wait. He had not the nerve to bear suspense nor yet to brave the crash of battle. So weakening his army by the withdrawal of his guard, he retired to Brixellum (Brescia), to wait impatiently for the result, and to send messages in quick succession to urge his generals to fight without delay. The armies met in the shock of battle on the plains near Bedriacum, where Otho's best generals, forced to fight against their will, were the first to leave the field, and his ill-led and mutinous

After fruitless overtures of peace,

Otho marched to meet them.

His generals urged delay, but he would not wait.

His army was routed on the battle field of Bedriacum,

soldiers broke and fled. But the poor gladiators stood their ground and died almost to a man. The fugitives from the field of battle soon brought the tidings to Brixellum, and Otho saw that all was over. His guards, indeed, boasted of their loyal love, and urged him to live and to renew the struggle, and told him of his distant armies on the march. But he had staked his all upon a single battle, and he knew that he must pay his losses. He was sick perhaps of civil bloodshed, though the fine words which Tacitus ascribe to him sound strange in the mouth of one who plotted against Galba and gloated over Piso's death. He waited one more day to let the senators retire who had reluctantly followed him to war, and to save Verginius from the blind fury of the soldiers, or perhaps with some faint lingering hope of rescue; he spent one more night, we know not in what thoughts, upon his bed, and at the dawn took up his dagger and died by his own hand. It was certainly no hero's death. The meanest of that day, the poor gladiator of the stage, could face death calmly when his hour was come; and reigns of terror and the Stoics' creed had long made suicide a thing of course to every weary or despairing soul. Yet so rare were the lessons of unselfishness in high places, that men thought it noble in him to risk no more his soldiers' lives, painted with a loving hand the picture of his death, and whispered that his bold stroke for empire was perhaps the act, not of an unscrupulous adventurer, but of a republican who wished to restore his country's freedom.

and he died by his own hand at Brixellum.

CHAPTER VIII.

VITELLIUS.—A. D. 69.

A. VITELLIUS had only a short term of power, but it was long enough to mark perhaps the lowest depth to which elective monarchy has ever fallen. His father Lucius had done good service as a soldier, but he came back to Rome to disgrace his name by mean and abject flattery of the ruling powers. To pay his homage to the divine Caligula he veiled his beard and bowed to the ground in silent adoration. To push his fortunes in the court of Claudius, where wives and freedmen ruled, he kept the effigies of Pallas and Narcissus among those of his household gods, and carried one of Messalina's slippers in his bosom, to have the pleasure of kissing it in public. He rose to be thrice consul, and the admiring Senate had graven on his statue in the Forum the words which told of his unswerving loyalty towards his prince. The son followed in his father's steps and pandered to the vices of three Emperors in turn. As a youth he shared the sensual orgies of Tiberius at Capreæ, he pleased Claudius by his skill at dice, and Nero by using a show of force when he was too shy to sing in public. In the province of Africa he bore a better character as proconsul, but as commissioner of public works at Rome he was said to have filched the gold out of the temples and replaced it with ornaments of baser metal. Yet on the recall of Verginius he was sent by Galba to command the camp in lower Germany. Men thought the appointment strange enough.

The antecedents of Vitellius.

He copied his father in mean flattery and complaisance.

Sent by Galba to command the army on the Rhine.

Some said he owed it to a favorite's caprice; some fancied that he was chosen from contempt, as too mean and slothful to be dangerous in command. He was the greatest glutton of his times, had eaten all his means away, and had to leave his family in hired lodgings and to pledge his mother's jewels to pay the expenses of his journey. But he started in the gayest mood, made messmates and friends of all he met, and did not stay to pick and choose. His low pleasantries and jovial humor charmed all the muleteers and soldiers on the road, and in the camp he was hearty and affable to all alike, was always ready to relax the rules of discipline, and seldom took the trouble to refuse a prayer. The army saw in him a general who was too liberal and open-handed to wish to stint them to their beggarly pittance and keep them to taskwork on the frontier. He would not try to curb their license or deny them plunder if they were once upon the march to Rome.

Glutton and spendthrift though he was,

he won the affection of the soldiers by his easy good nature.

Two leading generals, Fabius Valens and Alienus Cæcina, saw in him also a convenient tool, whose very vices caught the fancy of the soldiers, and whose name would sound well in a proclamation, but who was too weak and indolent to wish to rule, and would be obliged to fall back on men of action like themselves. Both wished for civil war on personal grounds. Valens resented bitterly the neglect of the good service rendered by him to Galba's cause; Cæcina had just been detected in fraudulent use of public money and would soon be called to an account.

Valens and Cæcina, being disaffected to Galba, stir the army and put Vitellius forward,

Within a month a crowd of soldiers gather at nightfall round their general's tent, force their way into his presence, and carry him upon their shoulders through the camp, while their comrades salute their new Emperor with acclamations. The legions of the upper province were already in revolt, and soon broke the idle oath of allegiance to the Senate and joined their comrades of the lower Rhine. The two armies under Valens and Cæcina pushed forward by separate routes to cross the Alps. Their track was marked by license and by rapine. The frightened villagers fled away; the townsfolk trembled lest their riches should tempt the soldiers' greed, or jealous neighbors vent their spite in treacherous charges, and were glad at any cost to purchase safety from the leaders. Cæcina was the first to front the foe, but was beaten off from the strong walls of Placentia after a vain attempt to storm it, which caused the ruin of the amphitheatre, the finest of the kind in Italy and the pride of all the townsmen. Valens, however, was not far behind, and the two armies once united crushed the badly-handled troops of Otho in the victory of Bedriacum, near the confluence of the Addua and the Padus.

who is soon proclaimed Emperor.

The march to Italy,

and victory of Brediacum,

Vitellius was in no mood to hurry. He was very well content to move in pomp and triumph on the road, or float at ease along the rivers, while his guards did the fighting. The provincials vied with each other in their eagerness to do him honor, and they found that the one passport to his favor was to provide abundance of good cheer. He was glutton and epicure in one. The countries through which he passed were drained of all their choicest, costliest viands, and every halt upon the way was the signal for a round of sumptuous banquets, which never came too fast for his voracious appetite; while his train of followers gave loose to insolent license, plundering

while Vitellius is feasting by the way.

as they went, and quarreling with their hosts, and Vitellius only laughed in uproarious mirth to see their brawls. The rude soldiers of the North settled like a cloud of locusts on the fair lands of Italy; corn-fields and vineyards were stripped for many a league upon their way, and towns were ruined to supply their food. Pillage and rioting took place of the stern discipline of frontier armies, and camp-followers ravaged what the soldiers spared. Even in the streets of Rome the quiet citizens stood aghast as the wild-looking troops came pouring in, the untanned skins of beasts upon their shoulders, their clumsy sandals slipping on the stones. But the soldiers were in no mood to brook a curious stare or mocking jibe, for a blow soon followed on a word, and bloody brawls destroyed the peace of the streets where they were quartered. Cæcina, with his cloak of plaid and Gallic trousers, had little of the Roman general's look, nor did men eye his wife with pleasure as she rode by on her fine horse with purple trappings. With them in military guise came the new master of the world, the soldier's choice, with the drunkard's fiery face and weak legs that could scarcely carry his unwieldy frame. He now returned in state to the city from which he stole away but lately to avoid importunate creditors. His first care was to pay honor to the memory of Nero and to call at a concert for the song that he had loved, as if he saw in him the ideal of a ruler. But the substance of power passed at once out of his feeble hands; the generals who had led his troops governed in his name, while Asiaticus, his freedman, copied the insolence of the favorites of Claudius. Their master meantime gave all his thoughts to

The entry into Rome of the wild-looking soldiers of the Rhine,

with Vitellius,

who let his favorites govern while he feasted.

the pleasures of the table, inventing new dishes to contain portentous pasties to which every land must yield its quota, and spending in a few short months nine hundred million sesterces in sumptuous fare.

But in the East Vespasian was soon in arms,

But he had no long time to eat and drink undisturbed. Within eight months the armies of the East took the oath of allegiance to Vespasian, and the legions in Mœsia and Pannonia, which had not been able to strike a blow for Otho, were ready to avenge him by turning their arms against Vitellius. The main army of the enemy, indeed, was slow to move; but Primus Antonius, a bold and resolute officer, pushed on with the scanty forces that lay nearest on the road to Italy, and reached Verona before a blow was struck. He might have paid dearly for his rashness if the generals of Vitellius had been prompt and loyal; but their mutual jealousies caused treachery and wavering counsels in their midst, and all seemed to conspire to help Vespasian. The air and luxury of Rome had done their work upon the vigor of the German legions, and their *morale* had suffered even more. The auxiliary forces had been disbanded and sent home; recruiting had been stopped for want of funds; furloughs were freely granted; and the old prætorians had been broken up and were streaming now to join Antonius. The Etesian winds, which were blowing at this time, wafted the ships towards the East, but delayed all the homeward-bound, so that little was known of the plans and movements of the enemy, while it was no secret that the forces of Vitellius were daily growing weaker, and that Cæcina was chafing visibly at the rising popularity of Valens. The fleet at Ravenna was the first to declare against Vitellius, for their admiral Lucilius

and all seemed to conspire to help him.

The treachery of Bassus and Cæcina,

Bassus, had failed to gain the post, of prætorian præfect, and was eager to avenge the slight. Cæcina, who was taking the command in the north of Italy, tried first to let the war drag slowly on, and then to spread disaffection in the ranks, and to raise the standard for Vespasian. But the soldiers had more sense of honor than their leaders. Hearing of the plot, they rose at once, threw Cæcina and some others into chains, and fought on doggedly without a general. The crash of war came a second time upon the plains of Bedriacum, where, after hard fighting, the legions of Germany were routed, and flying in confusion to their entrenchments at Cremona, brought upon the unoffending town all the horrors of havoc and destruction.

and second battle of Bedriacum.

Even amid the scenes of that year of strife and carnage the fate of Cremona sent a thrill of horror throughout Italy. So suddenly came the ruin on the city that the great fair held there at that time was crowded with strangers from all parts, who shared the fate of the poor citizens. At a hasty word from their general Antonius, who said that the water in the bath was lukewarm and should be hotter soon, the soldiers broke all the bands of discipline, and for four days pillaged and burnt and tortured at their pleasure, till there was left only a heap of smoking ruins, and crowds of miserable captives kept for sale, whom for very shame no one would buy.

Sad fate of Cremona.

Vitellius meanwhile had hardly realized his danger, till the news came of the treachery of Cæcina and the disasters at Bedriacum and Cremona. Even then at first he tried to hide them from the world and to silence the gloomy murmurs that were floating through the city. The enemy returned

Vitellius incapable and irresolute.

to him the scouts whom he had sent, but after hearing what they had to tell in secret he had their mouths stopped forever. A centurion, Julius Agrestis, tried in vain to rouse him to be stirring, and volunteered to ascertain the truth with his own eyes. He went, returned, and when the Emperor affected still to disbelieve, he gave the best proof he could of his sincerity by falling on his sword upon the spot. Then, at last, Vitellius summoned resolution to raise recruits from the populace of Rome, and to call out the newly-levied cohorts of the guards. He set out at their head to guard the passes of the Apennines, but he soon wearied of the hardships of the field, and came back again to Rome to hear fresh tidings of treachery and losses, and to be told that Valens had been captured in the effort to raise Gaul in his defence, and to feel that his days of power were numbered. In despair at last he thought of abdication, and came to terms with Vespasian's brother, Flavius Sabinus, who had long been præfect of the city. In a few hopeless words he told the soldiers and the people that he resigned all claims upon them, and laid aside the insignia of empire in the shrine of Concord. But the troops from Germany, who had felt their power a few months since, could not believe that it had passed out of their hands, and they rose in blind fury at the thought of tame submission. They forced Vitellius to resume his titles, and hurried to attack Sabinus, who, with some of the leading men of Rome and a scanty band of followers, was driven for refuge to the Capitol. They found shelter for a single night, but on the morrow the citadel was attacked and stormed by overpowering numbers. A few resolute men died in its defence; and some slipped

Tried to abdicate, but was prevented by the soldiers,

who stormed the Capital and slew Sabinus;

away in various disguises, and among them Domitian, the future Emperor; but the rest were hunted down and slain in flight. In the confusion of the strife the famous temple of Jupiter caught fire. All were too busy to give time or thought to stay the flames, and in a few hours only ruins were left of the greatest of the national monuments of Rome, which, full of the associations of the past, had served for ages as a sort of record office in which were treasured the memorials of ancient history, the laws, the treaties, and the proclamations of old times. The loss was one that could not be replaced, but it was soon to be avenged. Antonius was not far away with the vanguard of Vespasian's army. Messengers came fast to tell him first that the Capitol was besieged, and then that it was stormed. They were followed soon by envoys from the Senate to plead for peace, but they were roughly handled by the soldiers; and Musonius Rufus, of the Stoic creed, who had come unbidden with his calming lessons of philosophy found scant hearing for his balanced periods about concord, for the rude soldiers jeered and hooted till the sage dropped his ill-timed lecture for fear of still worse usage. Vestal Virgins came with letters from Vitellius asking for a single day of truce, but in vain, for the murder of Sabinus had put an end to the courtesies of war. Soon the army was at the gates of Rome, and scenes of fearful carnage followed in the gardens and the streets even of the city, for the Vitellians still sullenly resisted, though without leaders or settled methods of defence, till at length they were borne down by numbers, while the population turned with savage jeers against them, and helped to hunt them from their hiding-places and to strip the

and in the fray the temple of Jupiter was burnt.

Antonius entered Rome and slaughtered the Vitellians.

bodies of the fallen. When the enemy was at the city gates, Vitellius slunk quietly away in a litter, with his butler and his cook to bear him company, in the hope of flying to the South. Losing heart or nerve, he had himself carried back again, and wandered restlessly through the deserted chambers of the palace. His servants even slipped away, and he was left alone. Before long the plunderers made their way into the palace, and after searching high and low found him at length hidden between a mattress in the porter's lodge, or, as another version of the story runs, crouching in a kennel with the dogs. They dragged him out with insults and blows, paraded him in mockery through the streets, and buffeted him to death at last in the place where the bodies of the meanest criminals were flung to feed the birds of prey.

Vitellius was dragged from his hidding-place and slain, with insults.

CHAPTER IX.

VESPASIAN.—A.D. 69–79.

THE Flavian family, to which the next three Emperors belonged, was of no high descent. It was said, indeed—though Suetonius could find no evidence for the story—that Vespasian's great-grandfather was a day laborer of Umbria, who came each year to work in the hire of a Sabine farmer, till at last he settled at Reate. His father had been a tax-gatherer in Asia, and had taken afterwards to the money-lender's trade, and dying left a widow with two sons, Sabinus and Vespasianus. The younger

The humble origin and chequered career of Vespasian.

showed in early life no high ambition, did not care even to be senator, and was only brought to sue for honors by the taunts and entreaties of his mother. Fortune did not seem to smile on him at first. Caligula was angry because the streets were foul when he was ædile, and had his bosom plastered up with mud. He proved his valor as a soldier in many a battle-field in Germany and Britain, but fell into disgrace again because his patron was Narcissus, on whose friends Agrippina looked askance. Then he rose to be governor of Africa, and was too fair not to give offence; but his worst danger was from Nero's vanity, which he sorely wounded, by going to sleep while he was singing, or by leaving the party altogether. Shunning the court, he lived in quiet till the rising in Judæa made Nero think of him again as a general of tried capacity, yet too modest and unambitious to be feared. By his energy and valor he soon restored discipline and won the soldiers' trust, and was going on vigorously with the work of conquest when the news came of Nero's fall. His son Titus set out to pay his compliments to Galba, and possibly to push his fortunes at the court; but hearing at Corinth that Galba too had fallen, and that Otho was in his place, he sailed back at once to join his father.

Sent to command in Judæa,

he showed his skill, and won the soldiers' trust.

Vespasian's friends now thought that the time was come for him to strike a blow for Empire. The two rivals who were quarreling for the prize were men of infamous character and no talents for command, while the legions of the East trusted their generals and were jealous of the Western armies. The rumor was spread among them that they were to be shifted from their quarters to the rigor of the German frontier, to let others reap the fruits of war; and they began to clamor for an Emperor of their own. Mucianus, the governor of Syria, might have been a formidable rival, for he was brilliant and dexterous in action, of winning ways and ready speech, had moved among the highest circles, and won the affections of his soldiers. He was no friend to Vespasian, for he had coveted his post in Palestine; yet now, from a rare prudence or self-sacrifice, or gained over, it may be, by the graceful tact of Titus, he was willing to waive all claims of personal ambition and to share all the dangers of the movement. But Vespasian himself was slow to move. He had made his army take the oath to each Emperor in turn, and he thought mainly now of the war that lay ready to his hand. The urgent pleadings of his son, the well-turned periods of Mucianus, such as Tacitus puts into his mouth, the sanguine hopes of friends, might have failed to make him risk the hazard; but the soldiers' talk had compromised his name, the troops at Aquileia had declared for him already, and he felt that it might be dangerous to draw back. The præfect of Egypt, with whom Titus had intrigued already, took the first decisive step, and put at Vespasian's command his important province and the corn-supplies of Rome. The armies of Palestine and Syria rose soon after and joined the movement with enthusiasm. Berenice, Agrippa's sister, who had long since gained the ear of Titus, helped him with her statecraft and brought offers of alliance from Eastern princes and even from the Parthian empire. But Vespasian was still slow and wary. While Primus Antonius pushed on with the vanguard of his army from Illyria, not staying in his adventurous haste to hear the warning to be cau-

Titus and Mucianus pressed him to make himself Emperor,

and he consented with reluctance,

tious, Mucianus followed with the main body to find the struggle almost over before he made his way to Rome. Vespasian himself crossed over into Egypt to take measures to starve his enemies into submission, or to hold the country as a stronghold in case of failure. There he heard of the bold march of the vanguard into Italy, of the bloody struggle near Cremona, and of the undisputed march to Rome. Then came the tidings from the North-west that the withdrawal of the legions had been followed by a rising of the neighboring races, and that even Roman troops had stooped so low as to swear fealty to the Gaul. The Britons and Dacians too were stirring, and brigands were pillaging the undefended Pontus. Soon he learnt that the Capital had been stormed and his brother killed in the blind fury of the soldiers' riot, but that vengeance had been taken in the blood of Vitellius and his troops. Each ship brought couriers with eventful news, or senators coming to do homage, till the great town of Alexandria was thronged to overflowing. Still he stayed in Egypt, till at length he could not in prudence tarry longer, for Mucianus having set Antonius aside was in absolute command at Rome, and his own son Domitian, a youth of seventeen, who had been left in the city but escaped his uncle's fate, seemed to have lost his head at the sudden change of fortune, and was indulging in arrogant caprices. Titus was with his father in Egypt till the last, and pleaded with him to deal tenderly with his brother's wilful ways, then left to close the war in Palestine, while Vespasian hastened with the corn-ships on to Rome, where the granaries had only food for ten days left, and Mucianus had been ruling with a sovereign's airs.

and was in Egypt when his cause was won.

Meantime the rising on the Rhine was quelled. It

had its source in the revengeful ambition of Civilis, a chieftain of the ruling class of the Batavi, who had twice narrowly escaped with life from the charge of disloyalty to Rome. His people had long sent their contingents to serve beside the legions. Bold, brave, and proud of their military exploits, they were easily encouraged to believe that they could take the lead in a national movement of the Germans. The frontier had been almost stripped in the excitement of the civil war, and the scanty remnants of the legions knew not which side to join, and had no confidence in their leaders. To supply the waste of war fresh levies were demanded, and the Batavi, stung to fury by the recruiting officers, listened readily to Civilis. They rose to arms, at first in Vespasian's name, and then, throwing off the mask, frankly unfurled the national banner, to which the neighboring races streamed.

The rebellion in Gaul and Germany—its causes,

The Treveri and Lingones tried to play the same part among the Gauls and to lead them too against the imperial troops, who, half-hearted and mutinying against their leaders, laid down their arms or were overpowered by numbers. Some even took the military oath in the name of the sovereignty of Gaul. It was but an idle title after all. The mutual jealousy between the several clans and towns barred the way to real union among them, nor would the Germans calmly yield to the pretensions of their less warlike neighbors. Soon, too, the tramp of the advancing legions was heard along the great highways, for the struggle once over at the centre, no time was lost in sending Cerealis to restore order on the Rhine.

early successes,

The wavering loyalty of the Gauls was soon secured,

and it scarcely needed the general's proclamation to remind them that the Roman Empire brought peace and safety to their homes, and that even if they could rend that union to pieces, they would be the first to suffer from its ruin. To reduce the Batavi to submission force was needed more than words; but the strife grew more hopeless as their allies fell off, and such as still remained in arms were routed after an obstinate battle, in which a river's bed was choked with the bodies of the slain. The submission of Civilis closed an insurrection, formidable in itself, but most noteworthy as an ominous sign of the possible disruption of the Empire.

and speedy failure.

It was left for Vespasian on his return to heal the gaping wounds of civil war, to restore good order to the provinces, and to calm the excitement of the capital after scenes of fire and carnage, and the vicissitude of the last eventful year, which had seen three Emperors rise and fall. The city was beautiful again, and rose with fresh grandeur from the havoc and the ruin. The temple on the Capitol was magnificently restored, and all the dignitaries of Rome assembled in great pomp to share in laying the foundation-stone. The temple finished, they were careful to replace some at least of what had been destroyed within it. Careful search was made for copies of the treaties, laws, and ancient records which had perished in the flames, and three thousand were replaced, as in a national museum.

Vespasian restored order at Rome.

But while pious hands were dealing reverently with the greatest of Rome's ancient temples the forces of destruction were let loose elsewhere, and prophecies of woe upon the Holy City of Jerusalem were nearing their fulfilment. To understand the causes of the rising in Judæa it may be well to glance at Rome's earlier relations with that country. The first of her generals to conquer it was the great Pompeius, and it was on his forcible entry into the Temple that attention was directed to the religion of a people who had a shrine seemingly without god. Falling with the provinces of the East to the portion of Antonius, Judæa was conferred by him as a kingdom upon Herod, and Augustus afterwards confirmed that prince's tenure and added fresh districts to his rule. For it was a settled maxim of his policy to draw a girdle of dependent kingdoms round the distant provinces, and gradually to accustom hardy races to the yoke of Rome. In the case of the Jews there seemed to be good reasons for this course. They were soon known to be a stubborn people, tenacious of their national customs, and ready to fly to arms in their defence. They were spread widely through the Empire, in the great cities and the marts of industry; but men liked them less the more they saw them. They thought them turbulent and stiff-necked, and mutual prejudice prevented any real insight into national temper, or any sympathy for the noble qualities of the race. It is curious to read in Tacitus the strange medley of gross errors about their history and creed—monstrous fancies gathered from malicious gossip or reported by credulous and ignorant writers. It is the more strange when we think that he must have seen hundreds of the men whose habits and beliefs he unwittingly misjudged, and one of whom at least wrote in his own days to enlighten the world of letters on the subject. At Rome the Jewish immigrants were looked upon with marked disfavor. Under Tiberius we read that thousands of them were forcibly removed as settlers

The causes of the insurrection in Judæa, and earlier relations of the Jews to Rome.
B.C. 63—A.D. 66.

to Sardinia, where, if they sickened of malaria, as was likely, it would be but a trifling loss. In Judæa the caprices of the Emperors affected them but little, though they flew to arms rather than allow the statue of Caligula to be set up in their Temple. But hard times began when, under Claudius, the country passed from the dynasty of the Herods to the rule of Roman knights or freedmen. It was their misfortune to be exposed to the greed or lust of men as bad as the provincial governors of the Republic, while zealots, who mistook the times, were fanning the flame of national discontent. They bore with the vile Felix; but at length the insolence of Gessius Florus provoked a hasty rising, which spread rapidly from place to place, till the whole country was in arms.

A.D. 66. A hasty rising at Jerusalem spread widely till

The general in command of Syria could make no head against the insurrection, which carried all before it till the strong hand of Vespasian turned upon the rebels with resistless force the strong engine of Roman discipline. But the war which had begun in a hasty riot was persisted in with stubborn resolution. Towns and strongholds had to be stormed or starved into surrender, till the last hopes and fanaticism of the people stood at bay within the walls of Jerusalem and the lines of the besieging legions. Two summers passed away while thus much was being done, and the third year was spent in further-reaching schemes of conquest, and the beleaguered city was left almost unassailed. It was at this point that Titus was left in sole command, eager to push forward the siege and to enjoy the sweets of victory at Rome. But he had no easy task before him. The city, strong

Vespasian was sent to command the army.

The siege of Jerusalem was left to Titus to finish.

by natural position, was fortified by walls of unusual breadth and height, and amply supplied with water. Within were resolute men who had flocked thither from all sides to defend the shrine of their most sacred memories and the stronghold of freedom, and whose fiery zeal swept every thought aside before their duty to their country and their God. There were also others more timid or more prudent, who better knew the force of Rome and feared the zealots' narrow bigotry. Thus mutual distrust and mutual slaughter weakened the forces of defence. After long months of obstinate fighting, discipline and skill prevailed over the dogged valor of the Jews—the Holy City was taken by storm, and the great Temple, the one centre of the nation's worship, was utterly destroyed. It was said that Titus was grieved to see the ruin of so glorious a monument of art. He had no such tender feeling for his prisoners of war. The outbreak which Roman misgovernment had provoked had been already fearfully avenged. Jerusalem was left a heap of ruins, and its defenders were dragged in their conqueror's train, to die of misery and hardship on the way, or to feed the wild beasts with their bodies at the amphitheatres of the great cities on the road to Rome.

The obstinate defence

and utter destruction of the city and temple. A.D. 71.

When the successful general returned to Italy it remained only to celebrate the triumph of the war, and the Jewish historian Josephus describes, as an eye-witness, the splendid pageant, which was one magnificent beyond all parallel. The procession of the day began at the Triumphal Gate, through which for ages so many conquering armies had passed along in pomp. The rich spoil, gathered from many a ransacked town,

The triumph after the Jewish war, as described by Josephus.

was followed by the long line of captives, the poor remains of the multitudes which had been carried off to furnish cruel sport for the citizens of Syrian towns. Then came the pictured shows that filled the kindling fancy with the memories of glory, strife, and carnage; the battle scenes, the besieging lines, the dread confusion of the storming armies, the sky all aglow with the blazing Temple, and streams of blood flowing through the burning cities. With each scene passed a captive leader, to give reality to what men saw. Then came the sight most piteous to Jewish eyes—the plunder of the Holy Place, the sacred vessels which profane hands had feared to touch before, the golden table of the shew-bread, the candlestick, which may be still seen portrayed, with its seven branching lamps, by those who pass beneath the Arch of Titus. After these came the images of victory, and then the ruling powers of Rome, the father with the two sons who were in their turn to succeed him. Hour after hour passed away as the procession moved in stately splendor through the streets. At last it wound along the Sacred Way which led up to the Capitol, and halted when the Emperor stood at the door of the great temple of Jupiter. While he waited there, the chief prisoner, Simon, the son of Gioras, was dragged off, with a noose about his neck, to the dark prison not many steps away. There was a silence of suspense while he was there buffeted and slain; then the shout was raised that Rome's enemy was no more; the last sacrifices of the day were offered in the temple by Vespasian, and all was over.

The war thus closed was a legacy of Nero's rule, for the present government was one of peace. Happily the new Emperor was a man of different stamp from any of the Cæsars who had gone before. There had

The economy and homely tastes of Vespasian.

been fearful waste of treasure, and the Empire needed a good manager who would husband its resources, and a quiet ruler who would soothe men's ruffled nerves. Vespasian was not a man of high ambition or heroic measures. Soldier as he was, he was glad to sheathe the sword; but otherwise he carried to the palace the habits of earlier life. He was simple and homely in his tastes, affected no dignity, kept little state, and had no expensive pleasures.

Much of the cruelty of previous monarchs grew out of their wanton waste. The imperial revenue was small, and their extravagance soon drained their coffers; to replenish them they had recourse to rapine or judicial murder. Vespasian saw the need of strict economy. To maintain his legions and the civil service, to feed and amuse a population of proud paupers, and to make good the ravages of fire and sword, he needed a full treasury, and there could be little left to spend upon himself. But for himself he needed little. He loved his little house among the Sabine hills better than the palace of the Cæsars; drank his wine with keener relish from his old grandmother's cup than from gold or silver goblets; disliked parade or etiquette, and could scarcely sit through the stately weariness of triumphal show. He mocked at the flatterers who thought to please his vanity by making Hercules the founder of his race; and unwillingly, at Alexandria, submitted to test the virtue of his imperial hands on the blind who were brought to him to cure, as in later days monarchs used to touch for the king's evil.

Stories soon passed from mouth to mouth to show how he disliked luxurious habits. A perfumed fop, we read, came to thank him for the promise of promotion, but saw the great man turn away saying, "I would rather that you smelt of garlic," and found his apointment cancelled after all. But as ruler he never seemed content. He said from the first that he must have a vast sum to carry on the government, and he showed no lack of energy in raising it. Even at Alexandria, the first city to salute him Emperor, the people who looked for gratitude heard only of higher taxes in the place of bounty, and vented their disgust in angry nicknames. Fresh tolls and taxes were imposed on every side by a financier who was indifferent to public talk or ridicule, and shrank from no source of income, however mean or unsavory the name might seem, if only it filled his coffers. Men remembered that his father had been taxgatherer and usurer by turns, and they said the son took after him, when they saw their ruler stooping to unworthy traffic, selling his favors and immunities, bestowing honors on the highest bidder, and prostituting as they fancied, the justice of his courts of law. It was said that he employed his mistress, Cænis, as a go-between in such degrading business, and that he allowed his fiscal agents to enrich themselves by greed and fraud, stepping in at last to take the spoil, and draining them like sponges dry. The wits of Rome of course amused themselves at his expense, and told their stories of his want of dignity. A servant one day asked him for a favor for one whom he called his brother. The Emperor sent at once to call the suitor to him, made him pay him down the sum which he had promised to his friend at court, and then when the servant came again to ask the favor said in answer "Look out for another brother, for he whom you call yours is now

But he needed and raised a large revenue,

and imposed new tolls and taxes,

and made money in unseemly ways, at which gossips made merry.

mine." Another time a deputation came to tell him that a town had voted a costly statue in his honor. "Set it up at once," he said, and, holding out the hollow of his hand, "here is the base already to receive it." There was, indeed, nothing royal in his talk or manners. He freely indulged in vulgar banter, and was never, it is said, in a gayer mood than when he had hit upon some sordid trick for raising money. Of such tales many, perhaps, were mere idle talk, the spleen of men who thought it hard to be called upon to pay their quota to the expenses of the State.

The money was certainly well used, however it was gotten. Government was carried on with a strong though thrifty hand, and peace and order were everywhere secured. Liberal grants were made to cities in which fire and earthquake had made havoc; senators were provided with means to support their rank, and old families saved from ruin by timely generosity. The fine arts and liberal studies were encouraged; public professorships were founded and endowed out of the Emperor's privy purse. Nor were the amusements of the people overlooked, though his outlay on this score seemed mean and parsimonious as compared with the extravagance of Nero. It was the great merit of Vespasian that absolute power had no disturbing influence on his judgment or his temper. He had no suspicious fears, but let his doors stand open to all comers through the day, and dropped the earlier habit of the court of searching those who entered. He showed no jealousy of great men round him, and treated Mucianus with forbearance, though his patience was sorely tried by his haughty airs. He was in no haste to assert his dignity, and when Demetrius the Cynic kept

But the money was well used for public objects.

He was free from jealousy and suspicion,

his seat and vented some rude speech as he came near him, he only called him "a snarling cur" and passed on his way.

In one case, indeed, he was persuaded to take harsher measures. Helvidius Priscus, the son-in-law of Thrasea Pætus, had from the first asserted in the most offensive forms his claims to republican equality. He spoke of his prince by name without a title of rank or honor; as prætor he ignored him in all official acts, and treated him when they met with almost cynical contempt. He was not content seemingly to be let alone, but aspired to be a martyr to his Stoic dogmas. Vespasian was provoked at last to give the order for his death, recalling it, indeed, soon after, but only to be told that it was too late to save him, for Titus and his chief advisers felt the danger from the philosophic malcontents, saw how much their policy of abstention had weakened the government of Nero, and were resolved that Helvidius should die, though at the cost of Vespasian's regret and self-reproach.

Yet was persuaded to put to death Helvidius Priscus,

There was also another scene, and one too of unusual pathos, in which he acted sternly. Julius Sabinus was a chieftain of the Lingones who called his clan to arms for Gallic independence. The movement failed—the Sequani against whom he marched having defeated him. He heard that the Roman eagles were at hand, and in despair the would-be Cæsar burnt his house over his head and hid himself in a dark cave, in hope that men might think him dead. His wife Epponina believed he was no more, and gave way to such an agony of grief that he sent a trusty messenger to tell her all and bid her join him. For years she lived, in the town by day among her unsuspecting friends, and

and also J. Sabinus, in spite of the touching story of his wife's faithful love.

in the hours of darkness with her husband. She began to hope that she might free them both from the weariness of this concealment if she could but go to Rome and win his pardon. She dared not leave him in his hiding-place alone, so she took him with her in disguise. But the long journey was a fruitless one—the boon was never granted. Sadly and wearily they made their way back to their hiding-place, to carry on the old life of disguise and of suspense. Then, to make her trial harder, she bore two children to her husband. She hid her state from every eye, hid her little ones even from her friends, suckled and reared them for some time in that dark cave with their father. At length the secret was discovered, and the whole family was carried off to hear their sentence from Vespasian's lips. In vain she asked for mercy, in vain she pleaded that the rash presumption of a moment had been atoned for by long years of lingering suspense; in vain she brought her little ones to lisp with their infant lips the cry for pity, till the Emperor's heart was touched and he was ready to relent. But Titus stood by and was seemingly unmoved. He urged that it would be a dangerous example to let any hope for mercy who had showed such high ambition, and that State policy required that they should die. Unable to save her husband, the noble-hearted woman bore him company in death, and left the Emperor's presence with defiance on her lips.

Vespasian worked hard and died in harness.

Vespasian was soon to follow her. He had passed ten years of sovereignty and sixty-nine of life. His career as a ruler had been one of unremitting toil, and even when his powers began to fail he would not give himself more rest. Physicians warned him that he must slacken work and change the order of his daily life, but "an emperor," he said, "should die upon his feet;" and he was busy with the cares of office almost to the last. His jesting humor did not leave him even on his death-bed, and as the streams of life were ebbing he thought of the divine honors given to the earlier Cæsars and said, "I feel that I am just going to be a god."

The characteristic jest at his funeral.

Nor did the populace forget to jest in their sorrow at his death. When the funeral rites were going on, an actor was seen to personate the dead man by his dress and bearing and to ask the undertaker how much the funeral cost. When a large sum was named, "Give me the hundredth part of it," Vespasian was made to say, "and fling my body into the Tiber."

CHAPTER X.

TITUS.—A.D. 79–81.

The bright prospects of the early life of Titus.

TITUS was born in the tiny cell of a poor house at Rome, when his father was struggling on with straitened means. But when Vespasian caught the eye of the favorite Narcissus and was sent to serve in high command in Britain, his young son was taken to court, to be brought up with Britannicus and share his pursuits as school-fellow and playmate. His powers of mind and body ripened rapidly, and he gave promise of a brilliant future, till his early career at court was cut short by the murder of Britannicus. He was said even to have touched with his lips the poisoned cup and to have long suffered from the potion. Little is told of the years that followed save that he served with credit in campaigns in Germany and Britain and gave some time to legal studies, till his father took the command of the army in the Jewish war and the prospects of civil strife opened a wider horizon to his ambitious hopes. The memories of his early years spent in the palace may well have fired his fancy, and his adventurous spirit probably outstripped the slow caution of Vespasian. It was Titus who intrigued with Mucianus, who went to and fro between Egypt, Palestine, and Syria, who plotted and schemed with Berenice in the intervals of gayer moods, who compromised his father's name and drove him to come forward as a candidate for empire.

His ambitious hopes and intrigues in Judæa.

When all was won and Vespasian's strong hand was needed in the capital, Titus was left to close the war in Palestine and to pacify the East. The struggle dragged slowly on in spite of his impatience to return. His personal gallantry and skill in the conduct of the siege won the trust and affection of his soldiers; but his merciless cruelty to the conquered left a lasting stain upon his name. The winter months were spent by him with royal pomp in the great towns of Syria, where the Eastern princes flocked to do him honor, and alarming rumors spread at Rome of the sovereign airs which he put on, of the ominous influence of Berenice, of his unbounded popularity with the army of the East. Men began to fear that he would not be content to wait and share the Empire, but would rend it asunder in a parricidal war. Such fears were soon put to rest when in early spring he left his train to follow as it could and hurried with all speed to greet Vespasian with the simple words, "See, father, here I am."

Skill in the siege and cruelty to the prisoners.

From that time he shared in full the titles and reality of empire, assuming in his thirtieth year the Tribunician dignity which his father had till this time modestly declined, and dazzling Roman eyes with the pomp and magnificence of the triumphal shows. For Titus felt perhaps that Vespasian's homely vulgarity was out of place in the founder of a new dynasty, and that to balance the traditions of the Cæsars and the profusion of a Nero it would be prudent for the new rulers to do something to make themselves admired or feared. He had himself a princely bearing and a ready flow of graceful words; he excelled in manly exercises, and was a lover of the fine arts. He keenly felt the ridicule that clung to some of his father's ways of raising money, and urged him to think more of appearances; but in this Vespasian was not to be moved. He even bantered Titus on his delicate nerves, asking if he disliked the smell of the coins that were paid as the impost on unsavory matter. But in other things he was more yielding. He was willing to follow the imperial traditions and to spend largely on the great works which Titus raised to dignify the Flavian name or to eclipse the memory of Nero. The parks and woods included in the circuit of the Golden House were given back to their earlier uses. The palace itself was in part pulled down, and the Baths of Titus swallowed up the rest, while the Temple of Peace was built to hold the works of art which had been stored within it. The bronze colossus of the Emperor, founded for Nero by Zenodorus, was changed into a statue of the Sun, and gave probably its name to the Flavian Amphitheatre which still survives in ruins. In after years a triumphal arch was planned and finished,

He shared the imperial power with his father,

and studied magnificence of outward show.

Money was spent largely on great works.

on which we can still see the solemn pageant and note the great candlestick and other national trophies of which the Temple at Jerusalem had been despoiled.

Besides such tokens of imperial grandeur Titus relied, it seems, on sterner action; but in this he took his measures without concert with his father. He had managed to win his consent to the death of Helvidius Priscus, but Vespasian would be no party to a reign of terror. His son took the unusual step of becoming præfect of the prætorian guards, an office filled commonly by knights. The soldiers were convenient agents, who asked no questions but acted at a word; and if any one at Rome was too outspoken in his criticism or likely to be dangerous, he was easily removed in a hasty riot or a soldiers' brawl, or a cry could be got up in the theatre or in the camp, and the traitor's head be called for. In one case, it is true, treasonable letters were found to prove the guilt of a noble who was seized as he left the palace where he had been dining; but then it was remembered that Titus had a strange facility for copying handwriting, and boasted that he could have been a first-rate forger if he would.

Titus made himself feared;

If it was his wish to inspire terror he succeeded, for men already began to whisper to each other about his cruelty, and to fear that they would see another Nero on the throne. Still more unpopular were his relations with Berenice, which might end, it was thought, in marriage. Had she not already, like another Cleopatra, bound his fancy to her by her Eastern spells, and would he not probably go on to seat the hated Jewish paramour upon his throne? The populace of Rome, which had borne with Caligula's mad antics

and his relations with Berenice were so unpopular that he had to yield.

and Nero's monstrous orgies, were stirred with inexplicable loathing at the thought. Titus tried to silence the outcry with harsh measures, and had one bold caviller beaten with rods for a rude jest. But the storm grew louder; he saw at last that he must yield, and reluctantly consented to dismiss her. This was not all that men had to say against him. There were ugly stories of rapacious greed, of debauches carried far into the night, of sensual excesses better left unnamed.

Sinister rumors about him.

Such was his character at Rome when Vespasian's death left him sole occupant of the imperial office, and from that moment a change passed over the spirit of his life. Like Octavius he had been feared—he would now like Augustus win his people's love. The boon companions who had shared his midnight parties, the unworthy favorites whose hands were tingling for the money-bags which Vespasian had filled, the informers who had tasted blood and thought the chief hindrance in their way had been removed by death—all these vanished at once like birds of night when dawn is come, and were driven even from the city. He was full of tenderness and courtesy for every class, sanctioned by one stroke of the pen all the concessions made by earlier monarchs; said it was not a princely thing to let any suitor leave him in sadness with his boon ungranted, and complained that he had lost a day in which he blest no man with a favor. So scrupulous was he of any show of greed that he would hardly receive the customary presents; so fearful of staining the sanctity of his reputation that he aimed at universal clemency, and pardoned two young conspirators with a graceful tenderness for their

The change after his father's death.

His courtesy and liberality made him loved by all,

mother's anxious feelings, which made the mercy doubly precious. His father's strict economy had left the treasury full, and Titus could enjoy awhile in safety the pleasure of giving freely and the luxury of being loved, for the people who had feared a tyrant thought that the golden age was come at last, and soon began to idolize a ruler who refused them nothing, who spoke with such a royal grace and spent so freely on their pleasures. They did not ask if it could last, or if the revenue could bear the constant strain; they did not think that their ruler's character might change again when he had to face the trial of an empty treasury and a disappointed people. Happily, perhaps, for the memory of Titus, his career upon the throne was short. He had little more than two short years of absolute power, when Rome heard with a genuine outburst of universal grief that its beloved ruler had caught a fever on his way to his villa on the Sabine hills, and died, complaining that it was hard to be robbed of life so soon, when he had only a single crime upon his conscience. What that crime was no one knew. Posterity perhaps might think that his one crime as sovereign was the leaving the legacy of empire to Domitian, his brother, whose vices he had clearly read and weakly pardoned.

and universally lamented when he died.

Some great disasters mark in sombre colors the annals of his rule; in all he had shown for the sufferers unstinted sympathy and bounty. A great fire raged three days and nights through Rome; a terrible plague spread its ravages through Italy; and lastly, the world was startled by the horrors of a story so unparalleled in history as to tempt us to dwell longer on details.

The disasters of his time.

The volcanic energies had been slumbering for ages

beneath Vesuvius, or had found a vent perhaps here and there in spots higher up along the coast that were full of horror to the ancients, but seem harmless now to modern eyes. A few years earlier they had given tokens of their power by shaking to the ground the buildings of Pompeii, a city peopled by industrious traders. The Roman Senate, warned by the disaster, thought of removing the city to a safer spot; but the Pompeians clung to their old neighborhood and repaired in haste their ruined dwelling. The old town was swept away, with its distinctive Oscan forms, that told of times before Greeks or Romans set the local fashions, and a copy of the capital upon a humble scale, with forum, theatres, and temples, took its place. Some of the well-to-do migrated probably to distant homes and left their houses, to be hastily annexed to those of neighbors, who soon adapted them, though on different levels, to their use. But scarcely was the work of restoration over when the great catastrophe came upon them. The little cloud that rests always on the mountain-top expanded suddenly to unwonted size. The credulous fancy of Dion Cassius pictures to us phantom shapes of an unearthly grandeur, like the giants that the poets sing of, riding in the air before the startled eyes of men; but the younger Pliny, who was a distant eye-witness, describes the scene in simpler terms. He was with his uncle, the great naturalist, who was in command of the fleet then stationed at Misenum. Suddenly they were called upon to note the unusual appearance of Vesuvius, where the cloud took to their eyes the form of an enormous pine-tree. The elder Pliny, who never lost a chance of learning, resolved to start at once to

The eruption of Vesuvius a few years before

repeated on a larger scale.

The account of the younger Pliny.

study the new marvel, and asked his nephew to go with him. But the young student, who even in later life cared more for books than nature, had a task to finish and declined to go. As the admiral was starting he received pressing messages from friends at Stabiæ, close beneath the mountain, to help them to take refuge on shipboard, as the way round by land was long to take under the fiery hail that was fast falling. The fleet neared the shore, where the frightened families had piled their baggage ready to embark; but the hot ashes fell upon the decks, thicker and hotter every moment, and, stranger still, the waters seemed to retire from the beach and to grow too shallow to allow them to reach the poor fugitives, who strained their eyes only to see the ships move off, and with them seemingly all hope of succor. The volcanic force was doubtless raising the whole beach and making the sea recede before it. But Pliny was not to be discouraged, and landed finally at another point, where a friend had a villa, on the coast. Here he bathed tranquilly, and supped and slept till the hot showers threatened to block up the doors, and the rocking earth loosened the walls within which they rested. So they made their way out on to the open beach, with cushions bound upon their heads for shelter from the ashes, and waited vainly for a fair wind to take them thence. Pliny lay down to rest beside the water, while the sky was red with fire and the air loaded with sulphureous gases; and when his slaves tried at last to lift him up he rose only to fall and die. By a curious irony of fortune the student, whose great work is a sort of encyclopædia of the knowledge which men had gathered about nature, chose the unhealthiest spot and the worst posture for his resting-place, while his ignorant servants managed

The death of the elder Pliny. A.D. 79.

to escape. For the waves were charged with sulphur that escaped from the fissures of the rocks, and the heavy gas, moving along the surface of the earth, was most fatal to those who stooped the lowest.

The scene at Pompeii,

Meantime at Pompeii the citizens first learned their danger as they were seated at the theatre and keeping holiday. The lurid sky and falling showers drove them to their homes. Some hurried thither to seize their valuables and hasten to be gone out of reach of further risk; some felt the ground rock beneath them as they went and were crushed beneath the falling pillars; others sought a refuge in their cellars, and found the scoriæ piled around their dwellings. Hot dust was wafted through every crevice; noxious gases were spread around them; and thus their hiding-place became their tomb. Hour after hour the fiery showers fell and piled their heaps higher and higher over the doomed city, while a pall of darkness was spread over the earth. Then the hot rain came pouring down, as the sea-waters, finding their way through fissured rocks into the boiling mass, were belched forth again in vapor, which condensing fell in rain. The rain, mingling with the scoriæ, formed streams of mud, which grew almost into torrents on the steep hillsides, and poured through the streets of Herculaneum, choked up the houses as they passed, then rose over the walls, till an indistinguishable mass was left at last to hide the place where once a fair city stood.

and various forms of death and ruin.

The survivors returned and partially rifled the houses of the city,

Weeks after, when the volcano had spent its force, some of the citizens of Pompeii who had escaped came back to see the scene of desolation, guessed as they best could the site of their old homes, dug their way here and there through any hole which they could makeinto the rooms to carry off all the articles they prized and then they left the place for ever. Time after time since then the struggling forces have burst forth from the mountain, and the volcanic showers have fallen and covered the old city with a thicker crust, till all trace of it was lost to sight and memory. After many centuries it was discovered by accident, and the work of clearance has been slowly going forward, constantly enriching the great Museum at Naples with stores to illustrate the industrial arts of ancient times, and restoring to our eyes a perfectly unique example of the country town of classical antiquity in all its characteristic features. At Herculaneum there has been less done, and there is more perhaps to be looked for. It was a resort of fashion rather than a market town, was more under Greek influence, and therefore, had a higher taste for the fine arts than Pompeii; and above all it does not seem to have been rifled by its old inhabitant, from whose eyes it was hidden probably by thick coats of hardened mud.

of which all trace again disappeared.

The objects since collected.

More to be looked for at Herculaneum.

CHAPTER XI.

DOMITIAN.—A.D. 81–96.

DURING Domitian's early years his father Vespasian was hiding in disgrace. He lived in a little house at Rome so meanly furnished that it had not a single piece of silver plate, and his straitened means may possibly have tempted him to vice, as the scandalous stories of later days asserted.

Domitian's early life,

He first attracted public notice when his father headed the movement in the East, but Vitellius still left him unmolested. There was danger, however, from the fury of the soldiers, and he took refuge with his uncle Sabinus on the Capitol to see the fortress stormed and the defenders slain. He escaped from the massacre in disguise, and lurked for awhile in the house of a poor friend in a mean quarter of the town, But succor was near at hand, and the vanguard of his father's army not only brought him safety but raised him suddenly to unlooked-for greatness.

and danger from the soldiers.

The change was fatal to his modesty and self-control. He aired at once all the insolence of absolute power, gave the rein to his sensual desires, and bestowed all the offices of State at his caprice. Vespasian even wrote in irony to thank him for not appointing a successor to himself. The arrival of Mucianus, the vicegerent of the Emperor, put some check upon his license; but it needed all the statesman's authority and tact to temper the arrogance of the head-strong youth. The crisis on the Rhine was pressing, and they set out together for the seat of war, but all was over before they reached Lugdunum; and Domitian, detained from going further, is said to have sent fruitless messages to tamper with the fidelity of Cerealis. If he had ever seriously hoped to raise himself to the level of his brother he had quite failed, and he had gone too far to meet his father's eye without misgiving. To disarm the anger that he dreaded he feigned even folly and took to hunting flies, for the often-quoted jest of Vibius Crispus, that there was no one, "not even a fly, with Cæsar," belongs more probably to this than to a later time. Thanks to his father's tenderness or the entreaties of his brother,

Sudden change turned his head.

Kept in strict tutelage by Vespasian,

he suffered nothing worse than warning words; but Vespasian watched him narrowly henceforth, kept him always by his side, trusted him with no public functions, and flatly refused to let him lead the forces which the Parthian king had sent to beg for in return for his own proffers of support. But by this time Domitian had learnt to abide his time and to be patient. He hid his chagrin at being kept thus in the leading-strings of childhood, and took to poetry, coquetting with the Muses in default of graver duties.

he ill-requited the tenderness of Titus.

At Vespasian's death, however, the old temper broke out afresh. At first he thought of outbidding Titus by offering the soldiers a bounty twice as large, but wanted nerve to appeal to force; then he complained that he was kept out of his rights, as his father's will had named him partner in the imperial power, and to the last he tried the long-suffering tenderness of Titus by moody sullenness and discontent, and possibly even by plots against his life.

His power of self-restraint at first as Emperor,

His brother's death soon removed the only obstacle to his ambition and the only restraint upon his will. But, strange to say, wanton and headstrong as he had been before, he now exerted a rare faculty of self restraint, as if he were weighted with the responsibility of power and wished to win and to deserve the popularity of Titus. He spent some time in quiet every morning to think over his course of action and to school himself for the duties of the day. He saw that justice was the first requisite of social well-being, and he spared no effort to secure it. In the law courts he was often to be seen listening to the pleadings and the sentence given. The judges knew that his eye was on them, and that it was dangerous to take a bribe or show

and wish to rule well.

caprice. Even in distant provinces the governors felt that they were closely watched, and never, it is said, did they show more equity and self-restraint than in this opening period of Domitian's rule.

His treatment of another class showed a like spirit. The rise and fall of the informers had been a sort of weather-gauge of the moral atmosphere around. Since Nero's death the bolder spirits in the Senate had tried under each Emperor in turn to bring the false accusers to the bar of justice. The leading Stoics had come forward smarting with the memory of the friends whom they had lost, full of indignant eloquence against the blood-hounds who had hunted them to death. The infamous names of Marcellus, Crispus, Regulus called out an explosion of revengeful sentiment. The Senate even went so far as to ask that the old notebooks of the Emperors might be produced to furnish evidence against the men they hated. But little had been really done, and men thought they traced the malign influence of Mucianus in screening the criminals from attack. Titus had driven them away in disgrace; but now perhaps they were creeping, like unclean things, out of their hiding-places to study the new sovereign's temper. They could not be encouraged by the words that dropped from him: "The prince who fails to chastise informers whets their zeal;" nor by the penalty of exile fixed for the accuser who brought a charge of defrauding the treasury or privy purse and failed to make it good.

He discouraged informers,

He tried next to meet a growing evil of the times that was significant of misrule. He announced that he would receive no legacies save from the childless, and quashed the wills made out of vanity or ostentation to the prejudice of the natural heirs.

and legacies to himself.

Not content with such reforms, he tried to give a higher moral tone to the social life of the great city, to check the license of the theatres to discourage indecent pasquinades, and raise the respect for chastity and moral ties.

and tried to raise the moral tone of society.

Had he only ruled as short a time as Titus he would have borne as fair a character in history, and he would seemingly have deserved it better, for he grasped the reins with a firmer hand and wished to merit rather than to win his subjects' love. How was it that so fair an opening was so sadly clouded, or whence the change that came over the spirit of his rule? In the meagre account of ancient writers we find no attempt made to solve the problem. But we may see perhaps some explanation in the events that happened at the time. One thing was wanting still, the laurel crown of victory, to raise Domitian to the level of his brother. In an evil hour he coveted military glory, and set out for Germany, where a pretext for war was never wanting. But, high as was the order of his talents, he had neither the general's eye nor the soldier's courage, and his heart failed him when he drew nearer to the enemy. The German expedition ended as it began, in plundering a few poor villages, and in pompous proclamations to the army and the Senate. But far away towards the Danube there was the sound of the real crash of war. Decebalus, at the head of his Dacian hordes, was an enemy worthy of the most skilful generals of Rome. Bold, fertile in resource, and skilled in all the fence of war, he had drilled and organized a formidable power, which for years tried the mettle of the Roman armies. Hither also came Domitian to gain his laurels, and

The probable causes of the marked change of temper.

1. His complete failure as a general.

A.D. 84.

A.D. 86.

here too his courage failed him. He stayed in the rear away from all the fighting, while his legions, badly led, were driven backward in disgrace. Unwilling to return without striking a blow to retrieve his tarnished fame, he hurried to Pannonia to chastise the Marcomanni for neglecting to send him succor in the war. But thither also he was followed by his evil star. Instead of the submission that he looked for he found a vigorous defence; he was ensnared and routed by an enemy whom he had thought to find an easy prey. Sick of war and of its dangers, he came to terms with Decebalus without delay; and rare as it was for a Roman leader to conclude a war after defeat, he was glad to purchase peace at any cost, and to give not money only but tools and workmen to teach the Dacian tribes the arts of civilized life.

He could not face his people with the confession of his failure, so lying bulletins went homeward to the Senate to tell of victories never won, and to disguise the history of the campaigns. Honors and thanksgivings were voted in profusion. The imperial city and the provincial towns accepted the official story, and raised with dutiful joy triumphal statues to their prince. But the truth leaked out, of course, and Domitian returned to Rome an altered man. He read mockery in the eyes of all he met, detested their praises as gross flattery, yet resented silence as a censure. He gave costly entertainments to the people, but with a gaiety so forced and a mien so changed that men spoke of them currently as funeral feasts, till at last he took them at their word, inviting the senators to a strange parody of a supper in the tombs, and played with grim humor on their fears.

While he was in this capricious mood another even served yet further to embitter him. Antonius, a governor upon the Rhine, began once more the fatal game of civil war. Though he was soon crushed and slain, and his note-books burnt, to compromise no partisans, yet the suspicious fears of Domitian were not to be lulled so easily, and he fancied universal treachery around him. The plot was the motive or excuse for an outburst of vindictive feeling, which would not stay to wait for proofs, but grew ever more relentless the faster its victims fell. Like some half-tamed animals we read of, he needed to taste blood to reveal to himself and others the ferocity of his feline nature.

2. Conspiracy against him.

One further cause perhaps there was—a frequent one with vicious rulers—to tempt him to yet further evil. This was simply want of money. The fruitless expenses of the wars, the heavy price he paid for peace, the lavish outlay to keep up the farce and put the populace in good humor—these had drained the coffers which Vespasian had filled, and which the easy prodigality of Titus had already emptied. At first he was minded to economize by reducing the strength or number of the legions; but he feared to weaken the thin line of border armies, and in his present mood he saw a readier way to fill his treasury—the old, old story of these evil times. Fines, confiscations, and judicial murders, became once more the order of the day, colored at times by various pleas, but often too by none at all. He talked of conspiracies and treasons till his morbid fancy saw traitors everywhere around him; his suspicious fears settled at last into general mistrust as the hatred of the world grew more intense.

3. Want of money.

His numerous victims.

The Philosophers were among the first to suffer. Rusticus and Senecio died for their outspoken reverence for

The Philosophers.

the great martyrs of their Stoic creed, and many another suffered with them, till by one sweeping edict all were banished from the city and from Italy. Philosophy did not, indeed, make conspirators, but he feared its habits of bold speech and criticism, as modern despots are intolerant of a free press ; and he looked with an evil eye at men who would not stoop to Cæsar-worship, as persecuting Churches would trample out Dissent.

Apollonius of Tyana.

Among those who were brought before him at this time and banished with the rest one name is mentioned that may stand apart, that of Apollonius of Tyana. He was, it seems, a wandering sage, so renowned for sanctity and wisdom that a band of admiring scholars grouped themselves around him, and were glad to follow him from land to land. Strange legends of his unearthly power gathered in time about his name, and words of more than human insight were reported to feed the credulous fancy of the world. In the last phase of the struggle between Pagan and Christian thought the figure of Apollonius was chosen as a rival to the Jesus of the Gospels, and his life was written by Philostratus to prove that the religious philosophy of heathenism could show its sermons, miracles, and inspiration.

The generals. Julius Agricola.

These were hard times for earnest thinkers; they were not encouraging for men of action. Military prowess and success were too marked a contrast to the humbling disasters on the Danube to meet with much favor from the Emperor; but there were few generals of renown to try his temper. Julius Agricola is prominent among them, because the skilful pen of Tacitus, his son-in-law, has written for us the story of his life. His just, firm rule as governor of Britain, the promptitude with which he swept away the abuses of the past, the courage with which he pushed his arms into the far North and brought Caledonia within the limits of his province, form a bright page in the annals of this period. But they gave little pleasure to his jealous sovereign, who eyed him coldly on his return to Rome, and gave him no further chance of service or of glory. He lived a few years more in modest dignity, without a word of flattery, yet not desirous to court a useless death by offensive speech. When he died men whispered their suspicions of foul play, but the Emperor, who was named among his heirs, accepted gladly the token of his respect, forgetting his own earlier principles, or that, as the historian tells us, "only a bad prince is left a legacy in a good father's will."

A.D. 85.

But though he feared serious thought and action, the lighter charms of literature might perhaps have soothed the moody prince. In earlier days he had turned to poetry for solace, and the sad Muses, whom he had courted in retirement, had, as Juvenal tells us, no patron else to look to than the Domitian who had just risen to the throne. But the Emperor read little else himself besides the memoirs of Tiberius, and the writers of his day had but scant cause to bless his princely bounties. Martial, with all his ready flow of sparkling verse, his pungent epigrams, and witty sallies, had a hard life of it enough at Rome, and was reduced to cringe and flatter for the gift of a new toga or paltry dole. Statius, well read and highly gifted as he was with fluency and fancy, found it easy to win loud applause when he read his Thebaid in public, but gained little by his ingenious compliments and

Literary men.

Martial.

Statius.

conceits as poet laureate of the court, and had not means enough at last to find a marriage-portion for his daughter. Juvenal's appeal in favor of the starving Muses met seemingly with no response, and disappointment may have added to his high-toned vehemence and studied scorn. It was no time certainly for Tacitus to write without partiality or fear, and the condensed vigor of his style, its vivid portraiture and power of moral indignation might have been lost wholly to the world had not another Emperor come at last to combine monarchy with freedom.

Juvenal.

Tacitus.

Meantime Rome had grown weary of the bloodthirsty mania of its ruler, who loved to pounce with stealthy suddenness upon his victims, and to talk of mercy when he meant to slay. It was the rich, the noble, the large-hearted who suffered most in this reign of terror, and it was left to his wife and freedmen to cut it short. Finding, it is said, a note-book in his bed, and in it their own names marked down for death, they formed their plans without delay. It was in vain that Domitian was haunted by his warning fears, that he had his porticoes inlaid with polished stone to reflect the assassin's dagger; in vain he sent for astrologers and soothsayers to read the future; he could not be always armed against the enemies of his own household. The conspirators surprised him alone in an unguarded moment and dispatched him with many wounds, though he struggled fiercely to the last.

Domitian assassinated by his wife and freedmen.

CHAPTER XII.

THE POSITION OF THE EMPEROR.

AFTER studying the lives of the early Emperors in some detail it may be well to call attention to the marked peculiarities of the position which they filled.

The Emperor is virtually the source of law:

1. Henceforth the Emperor is virtually the sole source of law, for all the authorities quoted in the codes are embodiments of his will. As magistrate he issued *edicts* in accordance with old usage in connection with the higher offices which he held, as did the prætors of earlier days. When sitting judicially he gave *decrees;* he sent *mandates* to his own officials, and *rescripts* when consulted by them. He named the authorized jurists whose *responses* had weight in the nice points of law. Above all, he guided the decisions of the Senate, whose *Senatus consulta* took the place of the forms of the republican legislation.

he interprets the law,

2. He was called on also to interpret law, either in the ordinary course of his functions when he served as yearly magistrate, or as the high court of appeal from the sentences of lower tribunals, or through the Senate, which became a court of judicature for large classes of trials, and looked constantly for imperial guidance. We read often in the lives of the earlier rulers of the unremitting care with which they took part in such inquiries.

and enforces it, as head of the executive.

3. As the head of the executive the Emperor must enforce the law. Most of the officials soon became his nominees, though a few of the dignified posts were filled up with some

show of free election in the Senate; but the master of the legions holds the power of the sword, and cannot share it with others if he would.

His power unique in kind,

The power so expressed was unique in kind. It extended over the whole civilized world, over all the cities of historic fame and all the great nations of antiquity. It rested upon an overwhelming military force, and was met by no threat of physical resistance from within. Nor were there controlling influences to be counted on such as monarchy has commonly to face. Of political assemblies the popular *comitia* passed speedily away, and the Senate became the instrument of his will, consisting chiefly of his nominees, and never asserting the right of independent action. There was no power of privilege to face him, such as orders of nobility and corporations have claimed and held in other states. There was no powerful civil service or bureaucracy, such as can thwart while seeming to obey, and afford a potent but impalpable resistance even to a despot's will. There was no sentiment of public morality or national pride that he might not dare to outrage, for the people of Rome were a mixed rabble, swollen rapidly by slaves who had gained the boon of freedom, and recruited from every race under the sun. The men of dignity and moral worth might frown or shudder when Caligula played mad pranks and Nero acted on the public stage; but their displeasure mattered little if the populace were merry and the army loyal. Religion itself had no counteracting force, for at Rome it was a matter more of formal observance than of moral faith. It was not organized in outward forms to balance the authority of the civil power, and by a curious anomaly the Emperor was at once the highest func-

without check or balance.

tionary of the state religion, as supreme pontiff, and was also soon to be deified and to become the object of the veneration of the world.

It was a system of unqualified despotism, without ministry, nobles, church, or parliaments, such as it is impossible to parallel, such as was likely to produce the best and worst of governors, according as men were sobered by the responsibilities or maddened by the license of absolute power.

From the imperial will there was no escape. The Emperor might and did commonly observe the constitutional forms and act on the sentence of the courts of law, or he might dispense with such tedious formalities, and send a quiet message to bid a man set his house in order or let his veins be opened in a bath. A few soldiers could carry the death-warrant to the greatest of his subjects in a far-off land, and execute it in the midst of his retainers. There seemed no hope of flight, for only barbarians or deserts lay beyond the Roman world. But in return there was no escape for the Emperor himself. He could not weary of the cares of state, and lay his burden down in peace. There was no cloistered calm for him like that which Christian princes have sometimes found. He could not abdicate in favor of his natural successor; he must rule on, to be the mark for the dagger of every malcontent, and see a possible rival and successor in every great man or military chief.

There was no escape from the Emperor's power,

nor for him.

The Emperor's power, again, was based on physical force. It rested on no sanctions of religion, noble birth, immemorial usage, or definite election, for it was of revolutionary origin and took its very title from the power of the sword. Yet after

His power was based on military

force, but his policy was commonly not warlike.

Julius the early Emperors were not men of war, and had no military policy or ambition. They had every thing to lose and nothing seemingly to gain from war. The balance of the Empire might be lost while the chief was on the distant frontier, and a successful general might prove a dangerous usurper.

Little police force needed.

They seldom even saw the armies, for these were far away upon the borders, and at home there was so little need of armed repression that a handful of the city watch and a few thousand of the household troops sufficed for the police of all the central countries of the Empire. Municipal self-rule kept the towns contented; and though the nationalities had lost their ancient freedom they seldom showed a wish to strike a blow to win it back. In Rome itself the old nobility was little to be feared. They had no powerful following of clients or retainers, no rallying cry nor hold upon the imaginations of the masses; and their feelings might be outraged, their fortunes pillaged with impunity, if only the populace could be kept in cheerful humor and the prætorians and legions did not stir.

CHAPTER XIII.

THE RIGHTS OF ROMAN CITIZENSHIP.

The citizens of Rome a mixed race.

THE vast multitudes gathered within the walls of Rome were a motley assemblage of every class and race. War, proscription, and imperial jealousy had thinned the numbers of the old families of pure descent, and many of the great historic names had already disappeared; but early under the Republic complaints were made by the Italians that the attractions of the capital were draining the country towns of their inhabitants, and for centuries there had been a steady influx of provincials of every race; while the slaves of the wealthy households, gaining frequently their freedom after a few years of bondage, passed into the class of *libertini*, and left children to recruit every order of the state. There were still differences of legal status left between the children of the full citizen and of the freed slave, but the lines that parted them became gradually fainter.

But in what did the status of the citizen consist, and how far did the Empire modify the rights and privileges of the franchise? Of the civil law we need not speak. The rights of family life and property were specially determined by the old *Jus Privatum*, and only slowly changed by an admixture of equity from the Prætors' Edicts, and by an infusion of the wider spirit of Greek philosophy. The political privileges of citizenship were more directly modified.

Their rights and privileges.

1. Of these the earliest and most distinctive, the right of voting in the popular assemblies, became an idle form and passed away. After a few years the Comitia ceased to meet to pass laws or elect magistrates, for no representative system had been devised to collect the votes of millions scattered over the *municipia* of the whole Empire, and no statesman could regret the loss of the turbulent meetings of the Roman rabble which had disgraced the last century of the Republic.

1 Jus suffragii.

2. The *jus honorum*, or right to hold official rank, was still real and valued. It had not been an integral part

of the Roman franchise in the earliest days of the distinction between the *patres* and the *plebs*. It did not always go with it in later times, for we read in Tacitus the speech of Claudius in the Senate when some of the nobles of Gallia Comata pleaded for the right of office.

2. Jus honorum.

3. The right of appeal to the popular assembly, or *provocatio ad populum*, in capital trials, was a highly-prized defence against the magistrate's caprice, secured by the Valerian law, enlarged by the veto of the tribunes, and reinforced by the Sempronian law of C. Gracchus. But the Emperor now stepped into the place of both tribune and Comitia; he was the high court of appeal, and from him there was no flight.

3. Right of appeal.

4. The security from personal outrage or bodily chastisement which the Porcian laws provided had emphasized the difference of dignity between the Roman and the Latin, and continued in imperial days to be the constitutional right of every citizen, of Paul of Tarsus as of the inhabitants of Rome.

4. Immunity from personal violence.

5. The power of voluntary exile, of leaving Rome before trial in the law-courts or the Comitia, to live in some allied community, became meaningless from this time. The Emperor's hand could reach as well to Rhodes or to Massilia as to Tibur or Aricia, and the exiles of whom we read henceforth had been banished to inhospitable rocks for the most part by the sentence of the Senate or the courts, or sometimes by a message from the palace.

5. Jus exilii.

6. Freedom of speech and writing had been left large, but not unrestricted, by the Commonwealth. Scurrilous lampoons had been made penal by the Twelve Tables,

and the jealousy of an oligarchy dealt harshly now and then with petulant criticism. But orators in the Forum and the law-courts used the utmost license of invective. Augustus was careful at the first to do little to abridge such freedom, and to let men find in talk the safety-valve of passionate feeling. But when his temper grew soured with age, and the Empire seemed more firmly planted, he became more jealous of his dignity, and the formidable "Laws of Treason" were extended to cover words as well as acts. Spies and informers started up to report unwary utterances and garble social gossip. The praises of a Cato or a Brutus might cost the historian his life, an epigram against a favorite be avenged by his imperial master, and Lucan be driven to conspire when his verses had given umbrage to the tyrant. There was as yet no censorship of the press, no means of seizing some thousand copies of a journal before it had appeared for sale, no way of warping or poisoning the public mind by official lies and comments. Yet such freedom as was left lived by sufferance only, and despotism needed only more spies and agents and a more centralized machinery to be terribly oppressive.

6. Freedom of speech and writing.

7. Religious liberty was little meddled with as yet. Polytheism is naturally a tolerant and elastic creed, and a niche might be found for almost any deity in the Pantheon of the Roman ruler. Atheism itself was safe, for the state religion was a matter of forms and observances rather than of thought. If jealousy was shown towards any creed or worship by the statesmen, it was towards such as were exclusive and aggressive, like the Jewish and the Christian, leading, as they seemed to do, to turbulence and disrespect for established powers; or towards such as

7. Religious liberty.

were linked with sacerdotal claims, like that of the Druids, which might foster national memories and come between the masses and the Roman rulers ; or towards such as seemed of too extravagant and mystical a type, outraging sober reason or acting as hot-beds of secret societies and clubs.

8. Right of assembly.

8. The right of meeting was largely used under the Republic. The *contiones* or mass meetings of the streets were addressed by every great party leader in his turn, and no government had tried to put them down, except when they met by night in secret or led to open riotings. More permanent unions, called partnerships, clubs, guilds, and colleges, were freely formed, and most of these were recognized by law, and only interfered with when, at the end of the Republic, their machinery was thought to be abused by political wire-pullers and electioneering agents. Warned by such experience, the earlier Cæsars looked at such clubs with a watchful and suspicious eye, put down the newly-formed and barely tolerated the older. They feared, it seems, centres of attraction for the discontented, and secret societies that might meet under cover of a harmless name. But before long the restrictions were relaxed. Inscriptions show that vast numbers of such unions existed all over the Roman Empire, claiming on their face a legal sanction, connected with every variety of trade and interest, and recruited mainly from the lowest ranks—often, like the provident clubs of later times, with occasional meetings for good cheer. Formal history is almost silent on their humble interests, but the monumental evidence is full and clear.

9. The citizens of Rome claimed and enjoyed one further privilege, which the franchise did not elsewhere carry with it. This was the right to food. From

early ages the Government had bought up large quantities of corn to distribute freely or below cost price, or had fixed a maximum of price in harder times. C. Gracchus was the first to systematize the practice and let every household have its monthly allowance from the state at a sum far below its value. This was to be the Roman's salary for the trouble of governing the world. The step could never be retraced, though Sulla tried in vain to do so; the price was even lowered, and the corn was at last freely given. The first Emperors saw the dangerous effects of this—the discouragement to honest industry, the temptation to the idle and improvident to flock to Rome, the burden on the treasury of the state—but they dared not give it up, lest the malcontents should find a rival and a rallying cry; so they were content to scrutinize the claims and reduce the number to the narrowest limits and to confine it to the poorer of the inhabitants of Rome. 9. Right to food.

It was in this seemingly unlike our Poor Law system, that it did not at first at least imply as a matter of course the extremest poverty, for a noble Piso came, we read, to take his dole, saying that if the state was so reckless with its money he would have his share with the rest. It was unlike the French Socialist's "right to labor," urged of late years with so much vehemence, for it set a premium on vicious indolence and made the Romans the pensioners of the world.

CHAPTER XIV.

LIFE IN THE PROVINCES.

Great variety of political status in the provincial towns, and large amount of self-rule.

THE Republic had bequeathed to the imperial government the greatest possible variety of political conditions throughout the different provinces. As in personal status there were many intermediate positions between slavery and full Roman citizenship, so there were many stages of privilege and power between a humble village community and the mistress city. During her long period of conquest Rome had never tried to act on any uniform system. As state after state had been annexed she allowed the conquering general, with the help of a commission or instructions from the Senate, to define the political conditions of the country, and to lay down the *lex provinciæ*. The object of this was mainly to fix the amount of tithe and tribute, to map out the countries newly won into assize districts for the courts of justice, and to give or to withhold special privileges in the case of those who had been most marked as friends or foes. But the Roman statesmen were always tolerant of local customs, and had no wish for uniformity of system. They broke up, indeed, the political unions or federations which had been strong and might still be dangerous, but they respected the old forms of national life, and let their subjects manage their affairs for the most part as they pleased. Each country lived its separate life, with varying usages that had been slowly shaped in the course of ages, and every part of it enjoyed a large measure of self-government. Where the towns were all-important, as in states affected by Greek and Latin culture, there the old names and institutions lingered undisturbed. In Gaul the tribes kept something of their federal character, and the old name for the capital of each union outlived in many cases the one of Roman origin, as that of the Remi lives on still in Rheims. In Egypt the political unit was the Nome, and the laws of Ptolemy were still respected, as those of Hiero were in Sicily. The old Greek names of Archon and of Demarch often lingered on beside the official titles that were of Latin source.

The cities of the highest rank were *Coloniæ* or *Municipia*, whose citizens had either carried with them to new homes or enjoyed by special boon the privileges of the full Roman franchise. To this class belonged all the towns in Italy and Sicily and some few in the provinces. Next in order came the towns of *Latin right*, unconnected usually with the Latin race, but promoted to the rank which Rome's nearest neighbors and allies had once enjoyed. Here and there, too, were privileged cities enjoying by the bounty of Rome the rights of freedom and immunity from taxes as guaranteed by special treaty, and called on that account *free* or *federate* cities. Below these came the mass of *stipendiary* towns, subject to tax and tithe at the discretion of the Roman rulers, but administered by their own magistrates and little meddled with by the central government. Around each of these were often grouped a number of *villages*, *cantons*, *hamlets*, called by various names, and more or less dependent on the central town, of whose territory they formed a part, and by whose magistrates they were administered. Sometimes, too, wilder mountain regions were annexed in this way to the nearer towns, through which a civilizing influence might be brought to bear upon their ruder neighbors. In general, however, there was no marked distinction between town and country life, as land-owners and farmers were grouped together for mutual defence, and lived within easy reach of the community whose civil rights they shared.

Scanty reference in literature to the life of the provincial towns.

The ancient writers seldom speak directly about social life in any town but Rome. It lay outside the plan of formal history; its details were too well known to call for comment, and the national comedy, which must have thrown most light upon it, is now quite lost to us. The literary men could not live happily save in the capital. Though Juvenal speaks with bitterness of the trials of the poor client's life, yet he still trudged wearily about the streets to pay his court to his rich patrons, and kept his garret rather than to move to the healthy country towns where life was cheap. Martial spent thirty years of meanness as a needy parasite of fashionable circles, catering for their appetite for scandalous talk, and selling for a paltry dole his wit, his gaiety, and his licentious fancy; and when he went at last to his little town in Spain whose calm he had long sighed for, he spoke of it with disgust and weariness, and longed to be back at Rome again. Statius, again, grew tired of the city, where in spite of his poetic fame he could only get a miserable pittance by dwelling on the virtues of Domitian, and he determined to go back to his native Naples; but his wife was deaf to all his praises of the country, and preferred the Suburra and the crowded streets to the baths of Baiæ and the beauties of the charming bay. We cannot expect, therefore, to find in these writers much about the course of that provincial life which was so distasteful to them. Our knowledge on the subject is drawn mainly from the

Fuller details in the inscriptions.

inscriptions on stone and bronze of which so many have been found in different countries. From this source we may trace the efforts made to regulate the condition of the *municipia*, and to fix some uniform principles for the government of the most favored communities throughout the Empire. Thus, fragments have been found of what was probably the *Lex Julia Municipalis*, passed to regulate the choice of town councils and their magistrates. Two other laws found near Malaga a few years back date from Domitian, and go still more into detail about the constitutional features of the Spanish towns, from which they take the names of *Leges Salpensana* and *Malacitana*. Much may be learnt also from the funeral inscriptions, though indeed we should not glean much information of the kind from the grave-yards of our own times. But the old epitaphs seldom fail to note the local titles and honors of the dead, and tell us much incidentally of the nature of their rank and offices that would be otherwise unknown to us. To these, too, must be added the formal eulogies, the votes of honor, the thank-offerings and words of dedication, the records of the guilds and corporations, which, after being buried from sight and thought for ages, have been found in course of time in a rapidly increasing store. A whole city, too, Pompeii, has risen from the grave, to show us not merely the houses and the streets in which men lived and died under the early Empire, but the words even which their hands had traced, sometimes in stately inscriptions on their public monuments, sometimes in advertisements roughly sketched upon the walls, sometimes in the scribblings of school-boys or the careless scrawls by which the idle whiled away their time, and wrote out for all to read the story of their jests and loves and hates.

In the towns of the highest class the powers of administration were vested in a few magistrates, who held office only for a year. The chief of these filled the place of the consuls or prætors of old times, and were styled from their judicial functions *duumviri juri dicundo*, being also presidents of the town councils. Below them were the two *ædiles*, who, as at Rome, had a variety of police functions and the care of the streets, markets, and public monuments. Sometimes the comprehensive term *quattuor viri juri dicundo* was used to include both of the classes above named. There were also in the larger towns two *quæstors* to be treasurers of the public funds and control the statements of accounts. It was usual to take the census every five years throughout the Empire, and in the days of the Republic it had been the duty of the censors to preside over the work, and to carry it through with becoming ceremony and religious pomp. The Emperor took the censor's place at Rome, and no special officers or commissions were appointed for the purpose in the provinces, but the duumvirs of the year were charged to make all the entries of personal and real estate within the course of sixty days, and to send copies of the registers to the central record office. To mark the importance of the functions the honorary term of *quinquennalis* was added to the official tittle of duumvir, and as such appears often on the funeral inscriptions. It was the more prized as it carried with it also the duty of drawing up the list of the town councillors, as the censors had to do for the Roman Senate.

The executive officials: duumviri juri dicundo; ædiles; quæstors; quinquennales.

The town council, or *ordo decurionum*, consisted of the ex magistrates and others of local dignity and

The town council or *ordo decurionum.*

wealth, subject only to a few conditions stated in the municipal laws that have been found, such as those which shut out from office convicted thieves and bankrupts, or men engaged in trades regarded as discreditable, like the gladiator, auctioneer, and undertaker. A minimum of age and income was also fixed, but it was one that varied at different times and places.

A lucky accident has preserved for us the *album decurionum*, or roll of the town council of Canusium. At the head we find a number of titular *patroni*, for it was the usage of the town to connect themselves if possible with members of influential families at Rome, who might watch over their interests, and also to confer the honorary name on the most eminent of the local notabilities. At the end of the register came the names of some *prætextati*, or young men of high family, who were allowed to be present at the meetings of the council and train themselves for public life by hearing the debates. The councillors themselves managed most of the affairs of public interest, voted their local taxes, controlled the expenditure of their funds, made grants for public buildings, conferred honors, immunities, and pensions, and watched over the ceremonials of religion.

Popular assemblies still met for business.

But the popular assemblies of the citizens had not yet, as at Rome, become a nullity. In the inscriptions we can still read of the votes that had been passed "with the approval of the people." The municipal laws of the two Spanish towns, which may be fairly taken as types of the whole class, give full details of the mode in which the magistrates were named in public and voted for openly in all the city wards. The election placards posted on the houses of Pompeii show that the popular contests were very real and the excitement strong. At times even the women longed to air their sympathies; and though they could not vote they scrawled the names of their favorite candidates upon the walls. Sometimes party spirit was carried to such dangerous lengths that the Emperors were called upon to interfere and name a special præfect to take the place of the magistrate who could not be chosen peacefully.

Such offices were burden-some rather than lucrative.

If these municipal offices were hotly coveted it was only for the honor and not for any substantial advantages which they carried with them. Their holders received no salaries, as did the agents of the imperial government, nor had they lucrative patronage at their disposal. Their main privilege was rather that of ruining themselves to please the citizens. They had first to pay a sort of entrance-fee on taking office; they had to regale the populace on the day after their election with at least cake and wine, and often with more costly fare. The town councillors too expected a state dinner on a lordly scale; a present of varying amount was looked for by the members of every guild and corporation, and often by the citizens in general. The people grumbled bitterly if they were not amused by shows of gladiators or well-appointed plays. To secure re-election it was often needful to spend great sums on public works, such as roads, aqueducts, and temples; and, finally, to win the gratitude of future generations men often willed away large sums, the interest of which was to feed, amuse, or shelter for all time the citizens of the favored town.

In the less privileged communities throughout the provinces there was more variety of conditions, for the old institutions lasted on with the same names and many of the same forms as before the Roman conquest. The agents of the central government had a larger control over their actions, especially in matters of finance and jurisdiction and their consent was needed in all questions of moment. But they were too few in number to look much into details, and the towns retained everywhere a large measure of self-government.

Greater variety of conditions in the less favored towns, and large amount of self-rule.

Municipal freedom prevailed perhaps more widely than at any other period. Local senates met in council, magistrates were chosen by popular election, and patriotism, though confined within narrow range, was still intense. The inscriptions which are found in every part of the old Roman world, as well as the ruins of the great works which here and there are left, show us how real and widespread was the public spirit. The citizens vied with each other in their outlay for the public good. Temples, aqueducts, baths, theatres, guild-halls, triumphal arches rose on all sides, not at the expense of the whole society, but by the beneficence of the wealthy and the generous.

Public spirit and munificence.

Augustus set the example first, and urged his friends and courtiers to make a show of munificence in public works, and other Emperors were anxious to add to the pomp and brilliancy of the imperial *régime*. The wealthy and the noble copied the fashion of the day, which spread from Rome to the furthest provinces, from the city to the village. But the spirit of imitation reached much further. Roman life was a centre of attraction for the world, and exerted a levelling and centralizing influence before which local usages and manners passed rapidly away. The ruder races were drawn irresistibly towards

The attractions of Roman culture.

the customs of their conquerors. Their own chiefs tried in vain to check the movement. Roman pride put barriers in their way, and agreed at times to refuse the franchise and the speech of Italy to the new-comers, but in vain. The leaven of the Roman culture spread among them, and their national usages and laws and even their language tended rapidly to disappear. The wiser Emperors respected jealously the local liberties and traditions, and had no wish, in the first century at least, to carry out a uniform system. But Roman influence spread through many channels. The legions, as they passed along the roads or remained encamped upon the frontier, acted on the men with whom they were in daily contact. The traders who followed in their train carried with their wares the speech, thought, and customs of the central city. The governors and financial agents who came direct from Rome brought the newest fashions with them to dazzle the higher circles of the country towns, and gave the tone to social intercourse. The journals of Rome, or *acta* as they were called, were read in far-off provinces; the latest epigram passed from mouth to mouth; the finest passages of the orators of note, the latest poems of a Martial, travelled either in the governor's train or were dispatched in regular course of trade as literary wares to the provincial booksellers.

The liberal outlay of the rich lightened the burdens of local government.

As at Rome, the lower orders soon learnt to expect amusements ready-made, looked to the wealthy and munificent to give them shows and costly spectacles, and grumbled at their magistrates if they were not liberal enough, or if they seemed to think too much of what they gave. But commonly they were ready with their thanks; and if the largess had been generous and if the gladiators died with becoming grace, the grateful people passed a vote of thanks, or made the council pass it, decided to erect a statue in their benefactor's honor, but, as the inscriptions tell us, often let him pay for it himself. Liberalities such as these must have materially lightened the expenses of the local government. With no salaries for the chief officials and no costly civil service to keep up, no schools nor paupers to maintain out of the rates, and with so many examples of munificence among the citizens, the burdens of municipal taxation could not have been heavy. The towns had commonly some revenues from lands or mines or forests ; religion was endowed with its own funds, and the claims of the imperial treasury were moderate.

General well-being.

At the end of the Republic the burdens caused by war and confiscation, the merciless exactions of the governors, and the cancer of usury had spread bankruptcy and ruin throughout the provinces; but in the course of the first century of the Empire peace and order and settled rule had caused a widely-diffused comfort; the freedom of self-government secured contentment; and public spirit, feeble as it seemed in the ruling city, was lively and vigorous elsewhere.

Juster rule of the provincial governors.

The great boon of the imperial system to the world was the higher conduct of its agents as compared with that of the proconsuls and propraetors of the Republic. They were paid high salaries directly from the state; they needed not to ruin themselves by bribery and shows to win their places; they were watched by a financial agent of the government, and liable to a strict account at Rome before the Emperor, who had no interest, like their peers, in their acquittal.

It is true that if we think only of the numerous cases of extortion and misrule which we meet with in the pages of Tacitus we may believe there is little proof of better things. But the evidences of juster rule are real and solid. Oppression had been scarcely thought a stain upon the characters of the statesmen of the Republic ; but now even the sensualist and debauchee often seems to change his nature when he is weighted with the responsibilities of office. Petronius, Otho, and Vitellius redeem in part the infamy of earlier days by their clean-handed integrity in the purer air of a provincial government. The very frequency of the trials for misrule, which may startle us at first, is in itself a proof of the watchfulness of the central power, which was as vigilant with Domitian as with Augustus. The abuses of ages could not be swept away at once, and it must have needed time and vigor to convince men that the Empire was in earnest in the matter. The provincials themselves soon recognized the difference, and their literature speaks far more strongly on the subject than the Roman. Philo the Alexandrian, Josephus the Jew of Palestine, Strabo the geographer of Pontus, Plutarch the Greek, Epictetus the Phrygian philosopher, bear emphatic witness to the higher spirit of equity and moderation in their rulers. Countries not long subjugated show no wish to assert their freedom, though the legions stationed in their midst are mainly recruited from their own inhabitants, and become fixed to the soil which they defend and strangers to the Emperor whose name they bear.

Evidences of improvement,

The results, too, speak loudly for themselves. The impoverished cities of Asia raised themselves at once when the incubus of the republican governors was removed. There, as

and of real prosperity.

in other countries, the inscriptions abound in evidence of real prosperity. The cities adorned themselves with stately buildings; the rich, no longer afraid to show their wealth, used it with lavish generosity. Trade flourished once more when the roads were cared for and brigandage and piracy put down. Commercial guilds spread themselves over the world, and even the provident unions of the humblest classes gained a recognition and a sanction from the state.

But no guarantees of permanence in freedom and good government.

Men looked only at the present, and forgot that there were no guarantees of permanence in the municipal freedom and happiness now enjoyed, no lasting gain in the absorption of so many distinct centres of national culture, nothing to give dignity and independence to the provinces, as the federal or national unions had done; no security that the cautious, easy, and tolerant government of the present would not be gradually changed into the grinding machinery of a centralized despotism. They thought of their material blessings, and forgot the moral qualities that should make them lasting. They looked back with a feeling of relief at the turbulence of former days, at the evils done and suffered in the name of liberty, and felt with Dion Chrysostom, "Our fathers fought, as they believed, for freedom, but really for a phantom of the fancy, like the Trojans who fought in defence of Helen when she was no longer within their walls."

Thus it was in no mean spirit of flattery that they raised in every land statues and altars to the Emperors, to some even of the vilest who have ever ruled. Of their personal characters they often knew but little; and though dark stories of what had passed at Rome may have circulated awhile among the higher classes in the provinces, yet the people knew next to nothing of their vices and their follies, and thought of them chiefly as the symbol of the ruling Providence which throughout the civilized world had silenced war and faction, and secured the blessings of prosperity and peace, before unknown.

CHAPTER XV.

THE STATE OF TRADE.

The early contempt for industrial art at Rome,

To appreciate the influence of the Empire upon the interests of commerce it is needful to look back to some of the facts and feelings of earlier days. The Roman writers speak commonly with disfavor and contempt of the handicrafts and retail trades, and the common sentiment which they reflect seems to have grown more intense in the later ages of the Republic, at the very time when the tendency towards democracy became more marked. While the hardy life of the old yeoman was the ideal of the moralist and patriot, the work of the artizan or tradesman was a lasting stain upon a family name. This was due probably in part to the warlike and aggressive spirit of the old Roman policy, which relied chiefly on its husbandmen and shepherds to fill the ranks of its militia, while the industrial arts fell into the hands of the needy homeless aliens who were attracted to the city and could not serve among the freemen in the armies. The growing contempt for the weaker races of Greece and Asia heightened the dislike for the trades they filled and the work which they monopolized. But above all the

due to the warlike spirit which was fostered,

vast influx of slave labor that followed the career of conquest supplied living tools for every need, made manual work seem servile, and rapidly drove free labor out of every field. The tendency extended even from the industrial to the fine arts, and to some even of what we call the learned professions. The great Roman households had highly-educated slaves, who were trained to amuse their masters and to satisfy their æsthetic tastes. In old time Fabius Pictor had gained a name for skill in painting, but it would have been a discredit in a later age; and Pliny tells us of one of gentle birth who was mocked at and insulted for taking to the art. Roman dignity, says the same writer, will not stoop to practise medicine, but leaves it to the Greek and freedman. Slaves were trained to be actors on the stage; and much as the Romans loved spectacles, they could not themselves act without disgrace, except in the old Atellan farces, which, says Livy, were never *polluted* by professional actors. Education was mainly in the hands of aliens and freedmen, who kept schools under the name of grammarians or rhetoricians, and the same classes also supplied the copyists, librarians, and secretaries whose useful labors furnished the materials that were worked up by literary men of note.

and the influx of slave labor.

The contempt extended to professions and the fine arts.

But while the Romans disdained retail trade and manual labor, they had not the same dislike for commercial enterprise upon a larger scale. Soon after the Punic wars we may trace the rapid growth of a class of great speculators and contractors, who belonged chiefly to the second order of the state, the *Equites*, and whose objects were more financial than political.

Disdain of retail trade did not extend to commerce on a larger scale.

They followed the movements of the conquering armies, engaged to supply the commissariat, formed joint-stock companies for every variety of undertaking, farmed the revenues of the lands annexed to the Roman Empire, profited by the monopolies of commerce when the old federal unions were broken up and trading intercourse was suspended between the members, and came forward as money-lenders to advance the sums to be paid down in indemnities or confiscated by the governors' greed. At home they lent their money to the bankers, or bought up lands in times of cheapness, like Pomponicus Atticus, or had their slaves highly educated in industrial arts, or speculated in building-land, like Crassus. But their energy was of little profit to the world, nor did it further the legitimate interests of trade. It enriched Rome, or a few hundreds of its citizens, but it impoverished the provinces. It made wealth change hands; but it did not stimulate production or facilitate exchange or promote the growth of peaceful enterprise.

Growth of a class of merchant capitalists,

who enriched themselves without benefit to the world.

The influence of the moneyed aristocracy upon the central government had long been very great; and if trade had not been the gainer for it, it was not from lack of power on their part, but of will or insight. They could make their resentment felt by the few proconsuls, who were clean-handed themselves, and who would not stand by and see wrong done. They could protect in the Roman courts the more criminal and unscrupulous of their body. They could in their short-sighted jealousy strike down great commercial rivals, as in the case of Carthage, Corinth, and Rhodes; but they do not seem to have raised their voices to protest while war was destroying or weakening so many distinct centres of civilization and production throughout Italy, while injudicious taxation and bad poor-law systems were injuring industry, and sumptuary laws discouraging consumption, while roads were made rather for the transport of armies than for the interchange of products. They were never so strong a power in the state as towards the close of the Republic, when the corsairs swept the seas and organized themselves almost as a belligerent power, while on the mainland runaway slave-bands and professional brigands were infesting the highways.

We may now turn to trace the action of the Empire upon these conditions. When Augustus was finally seated in his place, it was his first aim to secure the high-roads of commerce, and to maintain safety of intercourse throughout the Roman world. He put down brigandage with a strong hand, appointing special officers to do the work and armed patrols to maintain peace and order. Inspectors visited the factories and farms in country districts, where the slave-gangs toiled in chains, restored to liberty many who had been kidnapped by violence, and returned to their masters some thirty thousand runaways. The highways were made safe for quiet travellers, though the satires and romances still speak of brigands from time to time, just as they are brought occasionally upon the modern stage. On the seas, too, piracy was put down, and almost banished for centuries from the Mediterranean, though in the Black Sea it was still a matter of complaint.

What the Empire did for trade.

It secured the roads and seas,

It was a greater boon to trade that war was confined mainly to the frontiers, among the scarcely civilized neighbors of the Empire. After Nero's death, indeed, great armies tramped across the central countries, spreading havoc

confined war to the frontiers,

and desolation in their track, but with this exception the soldiers were confined to border camps, and no fatal check was given by the horrors of war to peaceful enterprise and industry.

removed a variety of checks and hindrances,

By a series of further measures the Empire did its best to remove checks and hindrances to the activity of commerce. The careful survey and census of the Roman world under Augustus was one step to prepare the way for equalized taxation, and it was followed by others as important. Financial agents were watchfully controlled; legalized tariffs of the tolls and dues were made stricter to resist vexatious overcharge, while the courts of law administered more impartial justice between the official and the common subject. The old sumptuary laws which aimed at checking luxury and extravagance, were given up after a short trial and regarded as a mischievous anachronism. The endless variety of monetary systems which delayed easy intercourse between land and land soon ceased to inconvenience the world. Many of them disappeared, others were kept for local use or retail trade; but by their side one uniform standard was set up, and beyond all the various national coinages the imperial currency was the legalized tender which appears henceforth in official documents in all parts of the Roman world.

diminished indirectly the supply of slave labor,

Still more direct was the influence on sentiment which affected the social estimate of industrial art. Slavery had been the formidable rival of free labor; but the countries which in earlier times had supplied the most serviceable tools were now annexed, and only an outer fringe of barbarians was left to supply the slave markets by wars of conquest. The Northern nations furnished less pliant and docile laborers, whose work was far less lucrative than that of Greeks and Asiatics. As the sources of supply were being cut off, the fashion of enfranchisement set in, and the slave-born were set free so rapidly that laws had to be passed to check the growing custom. At the very time when the competition of slave labor was reduced, less scope was left to enterprise in what had been before absorbing interests. The old game of war gave fewer prizes, and the soldier's life seemed likely to be henceforth one of monotony and patient drill. The statesman's career was less tempting to ambition when the show of talent might be dangerous and stir the jealousy of Cæsar. The laurels of the orator soon faded when power passed out of the Senate's hands, and when the pleadings of the law-courts had no influence on the course of public life. But in the place of these interests of the Republic the early Emperors had tried to foster industry and learning. Julius gave the grant of citizenship to all who would practise liberal professions; Augustus encouraged literary labor through Mæcenas; and Nero, the artist-prince, weakened the old sentiment in other branches. In short we soon lose all traces of the feeling which prompted Cicero in his public speeches to disguise his familiar knowledge of the culture and the arts of Greece.

lessened the competition of war and politics.

The Emperors favored the higher branches of industrial art.

The currents of national sentiment could no longer flow in separate channels, as men of every people flocked to Rome. In Asia handicrafts and industrial labor had never been despised, and the gradual infusion of Eastern thought weakened the supercilious pride of Western prejudice. Something too was directly done by Augustus to give a higher

Influence of Eastern sentiment.

status to the industrial classes. A new office and badge of dignity was devised by the appointment of the "Masters of the Streets," a large number of whom were taken from among the artisans and freedmen of the city, to discharge certain police duties, and also to minister as priests in the little chapels raised in honor of the Genius of Rome and of the ruling Emperor. Guilds answering to this office spread, under the name of Augustales, through the towns, and helped to give organized force and self-respect to retail trade and manual labor.

The higher status given to industrial classes through the dignity of *magistri vicorum.*

It is still, indeed, a striking fact that there is no reference in Latin literature to any history of trade; nor do we hear of special treatises connected with the subject, though the works on agriculture were many. Nothing is said of the moral benefits of international commerce; nor, careful as the Romans were about statistics, did they connect them with the balance of supply and of demand. Yet under cover of the imperial *régime* a vast system of free trade began to flourish, such as the world perhaps has seldom known. Merchant fleets passed peacefully from land to land and exchanged the products of their different climates, while the central government was content to keep the police of sea and land, allowing tolls and harbor dues to be levied for purposes of local revenue, and watching over the corn trade with especial care, that the markets of the capital might be always stocked. But this trade was hampered with no theories of protection, and was not interfered with by commercial or navigation laws. The vast population gathered in one city required, of course, an enormous retail trade upon the spot; but there were few manu-

Without literary notice a vast system of free trade flourished.

factories upon a large scale near Rome. The necessaries of life came largely from the South and West, the luxuries from the East, while industrial wares were brought for the most part ready-made, owing to the greater cheapness of labor in other countries. The balance of trade was always against Italy, for she failed to supply herself even with food, exported little beside wine and oil, and had few great manufacturing centres. In old days the riches that had been gained by plunder and extortion went out again to seek investment in the provinces; but now that Rome was the queen of fashion and the centre of attraction for the wealthy of all countries, the realized fortunes came thither to be spent. The productive centres and the hives of industry were to be found in other lands—at Alexandria, which Strabo calls the greatest emporium of the world; at the flourishing marts of trade among the isles of the Ægean; or among the hundred cities of Asia Minor, whose industrial democracies had soon recovered from the pillage and misgovernment of republican proconsuls, and enjoyed a magnificent prosperity, with which no other land could vie.

Balance of trade against Italy.

CHAPTER XVI.

THE GROWING DEPOPULATION OF ITALY AND GREECE.

AMONG all these evidences of material well-being there were ominous signs to catch the watchful eye. The queen of cities had clothed herself in pomp and splendor; and stately villas, parks, and pleasure-grounds were spread over the

The ominous signs of depopulation.

country; but Italy herself grew poor in men, in moral energy, and in natural products. The culture of Greece had made its way over the world; but her cities of renown were sadly dwindled, and scanty populations lived among the ghosts of former glories. The heart of the Empire was growing more feeble, though the extremities were sound. Strabo, who travelled in Greece early in this period, gives in his geography a melancholy list of ruined and deserted towns. Ætolia and Acarnania were exhausted; Doris has no trace of her ancient peoples. Thebes was a poor village cowering within the walls of the old citadel; and save Tanagra and Thespiæ in all Bœotia there were only pauperized hamlets. Messenia and Arcadia were deserts. Laconia had not men enough to till it, and seventy of the hundred townships of old times were quite abandoned.

Strabo's account of Greece.

As early as the days of the historian Polybius it was observed that Italy could no more put into the field such forces as she raised in the second Punic war, and that not for lack of manhood but of men. The Gracchi not long after called public notice to the fact of the decreasing numbers of free laborers in the country, and tried to check the evil by sweeping changes in the tenure of land. Again in the first years of the Empire complaints mingled with alarm are heard on every side. Livy speaks with wonder of the armies that fought in old time upon the battle-fields of Latium, and says that in his day only a few slaves tenanted the lands that were once the home of so many hardy warriors. Pliny tells us of more than fifty towns in Latium alone that had passed away and left no traces, and of

Polybius notices the diminishing military force of Italy.

The Gracchi.

Remarks of Livy.

Pliny.

the ruins of old peoples that the traveller found in every part of Central Italy. Dion Cassius mentions the "terrible depopulation" which Julius Cæsar noted with concern, and the difficulty which Augustus found in levying troops to fill up the void made by the loss of Varus and his legions; while Pliny tells us of the grief and wounded pride which the same Emperor felt when he enlisted slaves in place of freemen.

Dion Cassius.

The stress which Augustus laid upon the remedies which he applied shows how urgent seemed the evil. He reduced, and would have limited still further had he dared, the number of the paupers on the free list of the state, to check if possible the drain upon the public funds and the great discouragement to industry. He drafted off his veterans into colonies and bought them lands in every part of Italy to recruit with healthy labor the decaying *municipia.* He provided an outlet even for the city populace, supplying them with land in settlements beyond the sea. Finding among the higher and middle classes a widespread dislike to the burdens of married life, he tried to bring legal pressure to bear upon the morbid sentiment, enacted civil disabilities against those who would not marry, and various privileges for those who had given legitimate children to the state. The laws Papia Poppæa were passed in the teeth of serious opposition; but, as we have seen, it was a current jest that the consuls whose names they bore were bachelors themselves; and Plutarch tells us that many married, not to have heirs but to become heirs themselves, since they could only receive legacies on that condition. What causes had brought about this ominous decline in numbers?

Attempts of Augustus to meet the evil.

1. The career of Rome had been one of constant war-

fare. The obstinate resistance of the Æquian, Volscian, and Sabine races gave a formidable check to the laws of natural increase. It was long before Italy recovered the fearful waste of life and means caused by the Punic struggles. To gratify the ambition of the ruling classes, to gain fresh lands for them to rule, the bones of the Italian yeomen were left to moulder in every country to which the conquering eagles made their way. The losses in the Social War alone are set down in the lowest estimate at three hundred thousand men, and are raised by some writers to a million. But, exhausting as was the constant drain of life, it was not too great perhaps for nature's forces to resist if others had not come also into play, whose influence lasted on when the Empire enjoyed at length a period of peace.

The causes of decline.
1. War.

2. The land-owners of Central Italy had been long unable to compete with the corn-growers of foreign lands. The stores of Sicily and Africa had been poured into their markets: the tithes paid in kind had been brought to the capital in natural course; governors had sent large quantities to be sold below cost price at Rome to keep her populace in good humor. Carriage by seat had proved cheaper than that by land over bad country roads, and free trade and the policy of the government together ruined the corn-trade of the husbandmen of Italy. The small proprietors or yeomen could no longer pay their way or hold their land, and were bought out by the capitalists who sought investments for wealth gained in subject countries. The small farms gave place to the great holdings of the rich, the "latifundia quæ perdidere Italiam," the vast domains which were the bane of Italy. Pasturage superseded tillage, and

2. Change from peasant proprietors to large estates, with slave labor.

slave labor took the place of free. A few wild herdsmen and shepherds wandering at large, with here and there a slave-gang laboring in chains, was all that could be seen in districts that had once been thickly set with thriving villages.

3. Slavery was doubtless wasteful of human life. In the Campagna of Rome, as in many other parts, unhealthy influences must have been alway near at hand, and malaria had to be met and combated. It was less dangerous when land was tilled and drained, and the constant experience and traditional remedies of the hardy natives enabled them to lessen or survive the evil. But slaves drawn from far-off countries, knowing nothing of the climate and its laws, guarded often by reckless task-masters and crowded in the unwholesome cells of the *ergastula* or work-houses, were less able to resist the ravages of pestilence, which spread faster as pasturage took the place of arable ground. For a time the loss of life was easily supplied from slave markets like those of Delos, where, as we read, fifty thousand human beings often changed owners in a single day; but they grew dearer as the boundaries of the Roman world included more subject races, and the voids were no longer easily or profitably filled up.

3. Slavery was wasteful of life.

4. The free population that had been driven from the fields betook themselves to the army or the city. The doles of corn, the frequent largesses, the shows and gaieties attracted to the crowded streets and alleys thousands who were too indolent to work but not ashamed to beg, and who could contribute nothing to the productive energies of the world. The country towns copied Rome as far as their means allowed, and attracted the idlers

4. Attraction of town life and discouragements to industry.

and improvident who lived upon the bounty of the rich. The veterans who had been sent out as colonists to settle in the deserted regions wearied often of the irksome restraint of the unwonted work, mortgaged or sold their little farms and.gradually came back to swell the numbers of the dissolute and needy populace, and lived as paupers on the pittance of the state.

5. Influence of vice and profligacy.

5. To these causes must be added the untoward influence of luxury, profligacy, and crime. Polybius noted the physical effects of the foreign customs that were spreading fast among the young men of the ruling classes, and pointed to it as a symptom of decline. The moralists and satirists of later days were full of passionate complaints of the luxury which they saw around them. These rapid changes broke down the moral safeguards of the past and gave free vent to morbid appetites. The spread of ease and license discouraged honest industry and weakened hardihood and strength of body. The sumpuous mansions of the wealthy, the fish-ponds, bird-farms, and deer-parks which reared luxuries for Roman tables, absorbed unproductively the capital which might have maintained multitudes of thriving husbandmen and turned all Italy into a garden. The riches of the world had been poured into the coffers of the ruling classes, but with little benefit to their own country, which grew poorer, while large sums flowed yearly back to pay for the costly wares and delicacies of foreign lands. Pliny, as a patriot, laments the steady drain of money caused by the silks and jewels and spices of the East But moralists said less of what called for far severer censure. Infanticide was widely prevalent, sometimes in the form of the destruction of unborn life, but more commonly in the exposure of the newly-born. It rested with the

father to decide if he would rear his child, and custom sanctioned the usage of exposure, though early laws had tried to limit it to monstrous births. The discretionary power was put in force most frequently in the case of female children, and passing references in literature show that they were often victims. Private charity sometimes reared the foundlings, and the inscriptions bear witness to the number of such cases, and leave us to imagine how many were exposed. Polybius had specified this among the causes of the dwindling numbers of the Greeks. Tacitus notes that the Germans looked upon the act as criminal; but he does so probably to point a moral, and is thinking of the vice of Rome. Still the usage lasted on under the Empire, and the Christian Tertullian brands the heathen of his day with the infamy of the practice then continued. In the Eastern provinces the usage was less prevalent. Sometimes religious sentiment discountenanced the practice, and often the spread of the industrial spirit and the vigor of productive energy gave a stimulus to the increase of numbers. Material well-being was diffused among the teeming populations of the commercial towns in Asia Minor, while the patriot mourned over increasing poverty in the western cities of the Empire, and the statesman had to recruit the legions from the nations most recently annexed.

CHAPTER XVII.

THE FRONTIERS AND THE ARMY.

THE limits of the Roman world in the first century of the Empire were well defined by natural boundaries. It spread from the Atlantic on the west to the Euphrates on the east. The Rhine and the Danube formed its northern frontier; while the sandy deserts of Arabia and Africa parted it from peoples almost unknown. It had been the special work of Augustus to provide an effective barrier against the races of the North; and at the cost of hard fighting, and after many dangerous campaigns, Pannonia, Noricum and Mæsia were finally subdued and the Roman arms were carried to the Danube. Nearer home the tribes that held the passes of the Western Alps were crushed after obstinate resistance, and many thousands of them sold into hopeless slavery, that the great roads leading to Gaul might be secured. In Germany tribe after tribe had been attacked, and Roman influence had been pushed forward to the Elbe; but the whole country rose in arms to crush Varus and his legions, and the boundary again receded to the Rhine. No attempt was made at conquest in the East. Even Armenia was left in seeming independence, and the captured standards of Crassus were recovered from the Parthians not by force but by diplomacy. Towards the south attempts were made to march into Æthiopia and Arabia Felix, but heat and drought alone were enough to baffle the intruders. Such were the frontiers finally accepted by Augustus, and recommended by him to his successors. In them, with

The frontiers well defined, as secured and accepted by Augustus.

one exception, no great change was made until the time of Trajan. But Britain, which had been only visited by Julius Cæsar, was further attacked, explored, and finally subdued in a series of campaigns dating specially from the times of Claudius, Nero, and Domitian, and thus furnished a sort of training school for the best generals of the early Empire. It was part of the policy of Augustus to leave a fringe of dependent kingdoms in the countries most recently annexed, leaving the people for a while to the forms of native rule, subject only to the payment of tribute or supply of soldiers. Of these the monarchy of the Herods furnished a well-known example, and many others are known in Syria, Cilicia, Cappadocia, Thrace, and Mauretania. But one after another, as kings died or dynasties decayed, these little kingdoms also disappeared; governors were sent to administer in Roman fashion, and the work of organizing went uniformly on.

Dependent kingdoms

Diplomacy and intrigue also were constantly employed beyond the borders; treaties were formed with neighboring monarchs to give an excuse for frequent meddling; dynastic quarrels were fomented; shelter was offered to princely refugees, and future rulers trained in Roman arts and letters. This policy was specially employed in dealing with the chieftains of the German clans and with the kings of the far East, and possible enemies were thus changed into friends or weak dependents. The early Cæsars prided themselves upon the success of their diplomatic arts, took credit for it in their speeches to the Senate, and stamped in this way a pacific character upon the policy of the Empire. For indeed, if we except the terrible crash of civil war in the year 69, the peace of the Roman world was scarcely

and diplomatic relations.

The pacific policy of the Empire.

broken for a century. A few border forays on the Rhine had their source in the wanton folly of weak rulers who thought to win a little glory upon easy terms. The Dacian war upon the Danube was left, after a few campaigns, for Trajan's energy to close; the national uprisings in Gaul were crushed with little effort; and in their guerilla warfare with the African Tacfarinas the Roman generals were only pitted against a brigand chief, who had to be tracked and haunted like a wild beast to his lair. Only when opposed to the desperate energy of Jewish fanatics and the untamed tribes of Britain were they called upon to cope with enemies who seriously tasked the resources of generalship and discipline. For the most likely rivals of the Emperors were the leaders of their troops. Of these the most adventurous were recalled often in their hour of triumph or warned to advance no further, and must have sighed, like Corbulo, "Happy were the generals of olden time!" for they were allowed to go on and conquer.

The standing army of Augustus, and the stations of the legions and fleets.

Pacific as was the imperial policy of Augustus in his later years, he had for the first time set up a standing army, and the forms in which he organized it were long left undisturbed. On the Rhine eight legions were constantly on guard divided between the higher and the lower provinces, and the defence of the northern frontier was further maintained by six more, who were siationed in Pannonia, Dalmatia, and Mæsia. Four held the lines of the Euphrates, two were needed for the care of Egypt, the granary of Rome, while an equal number held the rest of Africa. Three more were kept in Spain, some of whose wilder tribes had been but lately brought into subjection. These legions, twenty-five in all, were attended in the field by auxiliary forces of about equal numbers, bearing the names and national character of the races that sent their separate contingents to the field.

The chief stations for the fleets were at Misenum and Ravenna, on either coast of Italy, besides which the harbor of the Colonia Forojuliensis (Fréjus) was chosen by Augustus to receive some of the ships that fought at Actium. A few thousand men, nine cohorts of the prætorian guards, and three of the urban watch sufficed for the police of Rome; and elsewhere through the whole interior of the vast dominion no garrisons were needed, and the tramp of armed men was seldom heard upon the great highways that ran through the old countries of the Empire.

The legions themselves were seldom moved from the frontiers to which they were attached, but remained in permanent encampments, engaged in an unvarying round of military drill. Near the cantonments settled the traders, camp followers, and various classes nearly connected with the soldiers, and many an important town of later days derived its origin, and sometimes even its name, from the camp in the close neighborhood of which it grew. The legions were recruited from the border provinces, often from the very countries where their camp was fixed. In time many ties connected the soldiers with the peoples amongst whom they lived. Most of them had never even seen Rome or the Emperor whom they served. How strong an influence was exerted by the Empire on the imaginations of the peoples, and how substantial were believed to be the benefits of union, is found in the fact that so few efforts were seriously made to assert a national independence and call the native soldiery to rally round it. For the temper

The legions recruited from the distant provinces

were loyal and steadfast, and attached by many ties to their camps.

of the legions was in the main loyal and steadfast. The statues and effigies of the ruling monarch were commonly in the camp the objects of unquestioning reverence, and there at least Cæsar-worship was something of a reality and not a name. The military traditions of each legion acquired of themselves an attractive force over the fancy of the soldiers, and provident clubs and guilds for social union grew up gradually among them, as we learn from inscriptions found in Algeria after the lapse of ages. They were also encouraged to deposit their savings in a sort of bank set up in their quarters, the funds of which were large enough to provide the needful means for the rising of Antonius against Domitian.

The moral qualities fostered in the camps by

The camps were also the best training-schools for the old-fashioned virtues of faithfulness, straightforwardness, and hardihood, and in them were to be found the best types of the old Roman character, which, as moralists complained, were to be found elsewhere no more. If the funds of a country town had fallen into disorder, or uprightness was needed for a special post, the curator chosen by the government was often an old soldier, who had long been tried and trusted; and early Christian history throws, incidentally, a favorable light upon the moral qualities of the Roman officer. Those qualities were mainly formed by thoroughness of work and discipline.

work

Besides the mere routine of drill, and all the exercises of a soldier's trade, the earthworks and intrenchments of the camp, there was no lack of constant labor. Their armies raised the great highways through miles of swamp and forest, spanned the streams and bridges, built dykes and aqueducts and baths, and taught the border races as much of the arts of peace as of the methods and appliances of war. To save them from the monotony of garrison life and the temptations of unlettered leisure they had for the twenty years which was their minimum of service, a healthy variety of useful work to call out their energy and skill.

The second requisite of discipline varied more with the temper of the general in command. It was a singular feature of the first Cæsar's habits of command that he was careless of common rules, and allowed much license to his troops, saying that "his men, perfumed as they were, could fight." But his successors could not rely on the prestige of genius to inspire *morale*, nor quell their mutinous soldiers with a word, and they drew the bands of discipline more tightly. The greatest generals were commonly the strictest, and themselves set, like Corbulo and Agricola, a marked example to their men. The worst, like Vitellius in his few weeks of command upon the Rhine, were lax and careless, and rapidly demoralized their armies.

and discipline.

Next to the generals the most important influence on the temper of the soldiers was that of the centurions, for they might be harsh and overbearing and sorely try the patience of the men below them. They might be venal and exacting, and allow some to buy discharge from the common duties of the camp, while unfairly burdening others. They might be quite incapable and owe their places to favor rather than to actual merit.

Twice in the course of the period before us we have the spectacle of a complete breakdown of military discipline, and it is instructive to compare the facts of each The first followed close on the succession of Tiberius. Both

Two examples of the breakdown of discipline.

on the Rhine and in Pannonia the soldiers were in open mutiny, incited seemingly by the men who had most lately joined the standards, recruited from the city populace after the fatal loss of Varus. The complaints put into their mouths are those of men who chafed at the stern drill of camp after the pleasures of the capital, who found the strictness of the centurions hard to bear, and looked forward with despair to twenty years of service, remembering the higher pay of the favored prætorians and their shorter term of years. The second was in the troublous year of 69, when so many rivals struggled for the post of honor. The armies had to assert their liberty of choice by naming each their Emperor, and the sources of discipline were thereby disturbed, while the drill and work of stationary quarters were suddenly exchanged for the license and the plunder of campaigns. They constantly broke out in mutiny against their leaders, and complained that the centurions were harsh or cruel; and twice when they had made an Emperor they would not be denied the privilege of choosing all their officers at their caprice.

But these were the rare exceptions of exciting times, and the legions commonly were loyal, and the Emperors, careful of their welfare. They rarely received, indeed, the donative which the guards of the capital could almost extort at the accession of a ruler; but besides the pay, which was in itself a great burden on the imperial revenue, a special fund was formed in a sort of military chest to furnish pensions for the veterans who were discharged, and new sources of income were devised to meet the need in the form of a succession duty of five per cent. and of certain tolls levied in the markets. After the civil wars it had been common to plant military colonies, and to find land

The pay and pensions of the soldiers

for all the veterans. But it was found in time that they were sorry settlers and little suited to field-work, and the land passed speedily out of their hands. The system of pensions was, therefore, adopted in its stead. One further privilege we hear of, though only from the evidence of inscriptions graven on metal tablets found in various lands. They are the certified copies of the official document in which an honorable discharge was granted to deserving soldiers after the full term of service. It carried with it the full franchise to the provincials who filled the legions, and gave a Roman status to the worthy, as the Emperor's favor or a master's whim did to large numbers of a different class.

and *missio honesta.*

CHAPTER XVIII.

THE MORAL STANDARD OF THE AGE.

IF we think only of the most familiar of the social features of this period we may well form a low estimate of its moral worth, and say with Horace that the men of his day were worse than the generation that had gone before, and were to be followed by an age still viler. The fearful spectacles of vice seated in high places with the Cæsars: the sombre pages in which Tacitus portrays the selfish, cowardly, and luxurious nobles, vieing with each other in their praises of the rulers who were slaughtering them meantime as sheep; the passionate invectives of Juvenal, which imply that modesty and truth and honor had winged their

The natural tendency to believe that there was a moral decline in the first century of the Empire.

flight to other worlds, and left the Roman in disgust to men without dignity and women without shame; the epigrams of Martial, which reveal the gross profligacy of the social circles which they were written to amuse; the novels of Petronius and Apuleius, reflecting the lewdness and the baseness of every class in turn; and, weightiest witness of them all, the terrible indictment of the heathen world in the letters of St. Paul—these and other literary evidences are often thought enough to prove a moral decline in the early ages of the Empire. They may be also thought to show the demoralizing influence of despotism on men who in early days would have spent their lives in the public service, but who, losing their self-respect when freedom failed, turned to material pleasures to fill the void which politics had left. But before we accept such sweeping charges there are some pleas that may be urged, and should be weighed, in favor of a somewhat different conclusion. Satire can never be accepted as a fair portraiture of social manners. It dwells only on the bad side of life, and ignores the brighter and the nobler scenes. It may be, though it rarely is, accurate and exact in what it says, but good and evil are so blended in all our motives, thoughts, and actions that the pen which draws only the evil out to view must needs distort and falsify all the complexities of our human life. Or if it tries, as it sometimes does, to paint the fairer scenes as a contrast to the darker, it isolates and overcolors, and so destroys the naturalness of both alike, as when the Roman writers found a foil for the vices of the city in the healthy simplicity of country life, of ancient manners or of barbarous peoples. But satire may be taken to show a more searching spirit of inquiry a keener sense of the follies and vices of the age, a social

But (1) satire is not fair evidence.

unrest and discontent which point to a higher moral standard and may be the prelude to reform.

2. Juvenal was too vehement to be fair.

Juvenal himself, from whom our popular estimate is mostly taken, was too vehement to be accurate and fair. Soured, seemingly, by neglect and disappointment, struggling with poverty, though conscious of high talents, he fiercely declaims against the world that could not recognize his merits, and he is not very careful of justice or consistency. Each public scandal of the times, the profligate woman, the lewd paramour, the insolent upstart, the wealthy rogue, the pampered favorite of fortune, become at once the types of classes, and are so generalized as to cover almost all the society of Rome.

3. Literature deals with Roman life.

Nor must it be forgotten that most of the literary evidences before us—satirists, historians, and moralists alike—reflect the life of a great city, and tell us little of the average morality of the Roman world. It was in that city that the Cæsars paraded visibly the foul examples of their insolent license, and the temper of the court gave the tone to the social fashions of the capital. It was there that degradation entered into the soul of the high-born, and drove them to forget the cares and shame of public life in the refinements of mere self-indulgence. It was there that the great extremes of poverty and wealth lived side by side with the least sense of mutual duty and mutual respect. The great fortunes of the world came to the centre of fashion to be spent, while the proletariat lived upon its public pittance or scrambled for their patrons' dole. It was there that the old moral safeguards of local religion, public sentiment, and national feeling had been most completely broken down in a motley aggregate of people to which every race had sent its quota. It was there that slavery reacted with most fatal force upon the temper of the master, and through the multitude of freedmen stamped upon the city populace the characteristic vices of the slave.

In such a capital there was no lack of material for satire, and earnest minds were justified, perhaps, in thinking that the inhabitants of Rome had never been so idle, dissolute, and corrupt. Politics had dwindled to the scandals of court gossip, and the sterner game of war, with its hardy virtues and its self-denial, had passed into the hands of provincials far away. The craving for fierce excitement might be sated by the sport with the wild beasts, and the poor gladiators might fight and bleed to show the Romans how their forefathers had died. But there was much in the life of the great city that was exceptionally morbid, and we surely must be careful before we generalize what we read about it.

4. Complaints about luxury need to be carefully weighed.

The satirists of the Empire dwell with special force upon the increase of luxury in their time, and the spread of peace and of material ease caused without doubt a larger outlay on all sides. But the luxuries of one age seem the necessaries of the next. Civilized progress consists largely in changing and multiplying our common wants, the moral estimate of which varies with the standard of the times. If the animal nature is not pampered at the expense of the moral character and high thought, if the few do not unproductively consume the produce of the work of thousands, the moralist need not quarrel with the enlargement of our human needs, which of itself becomes a spur to quickened industry. But some of the complaints in question deal with matters of passing sentiment and prejudice, with entirely conventional habits of dress and food and furniture, and their strictures on these points sound meaningless to modern ears. Even the things we look upon as the real gains of progress, such as the interchange of natural products, the suiting to fresh soils and climates the growth of widely different lands, they stigmatized as the vanity of an insane ambition that would overleap the bounds of nature. Much of what seemed to them luxurious excess would be now taken as a matter of course, and was only thought extravagant because of the simpler habits of a Southern race, which had a lower standard for its wants. For if we go into details there is little that exceeds or even rivals the expenditure of later times, unless, perhaps, we may except the prices given for works of fine art, or the passion for building, which, for a time, seized the Roman nobles, or eccentricities of morbid fancy as rare as they were portentous. Wealth was confined, indeed, within few hands; but in the towns at least they spent largely for what they thought the common good, and baths and aqueducts, roads and temples were works to benefit the million. Culpable luxury, indeed, there was—selfish extravagance and idle waste—but every age has seen the same in all the great cities of the world. It is fair also to remember that the first century of the Empire had not passed away before a change is noticed for the better. We read in Tacitus that Vespasian's frugal habits had a lasting influence on the tone of Roman fashion. From his days he dates the spread of homelier ways, in which men followed the example of the court, while the provincials, from whom the Senate was largely recruited at the time, brought to the capital the inexpensive forms of simpler life. With these reserves we may accept the statements of the ancient writers for some at least of the social features of imperial Rome, for the vices and the follies which they paint in such dark colors.

But there is another side to be considered before a conclusion can be drawn.

5 Philosophy became a great moral power.

The case of Seneca.

Philosophy had now become, for the first time in Roman history, a real power in common life, and where Christian influences were unknown it was the chief moral teacher of mankind. With Cicero it had given an uncertain sound, as if to excuse his own irresolute temper; it had furnished questions of interest for curious scholars, but no guiding star for earnest seekers. But in the mouths of the great teachers of the Stoic system it was very resolute and stern. It pointed to a higher standard than the will of any living Cæsar; it taught men to live with self-respect and to face death with calm composure. It had dropped its airs of paradox and the subtleties of nice disputes to become intensely practical and moral, to lead men in the path of duty, and give them light in hours of darkness. It is easy, indeed, to point to the inconsistencies of a career like that of Seneca, to the moralist defending the worst act of his royal pupil, to the rich man writing specious phrases in favor of homely poverty, to the ascetic training of the hard wallet amid all the splendors of the palace, like the hair shirt of the middle ages covered by the prelate's robe. But Seneca found strength and solace in the lessons of philosophy; the greatness of his life begins when honors and court favor fail him, and he retires to meditate on the real goods of life and the great principles of duty. There, with a little company of chosen spirits, he can consult the books of the undying dead, and tranquilly reason on the experience of the past and the problems of man's destiny.

Not content with the mere selfish object of saving his own soul, he gives his ear and earnest thoughts to the needs of other seekers round him, writes as the director of their conscience while they live still in the busy world, and tells them how to keep a brave and quiet heart among the trials of those evil days. The pages in which Tacitus describes the last hours of Seneca and many another death-bed scene; the marked way in which he comments on the worldly levity of Petronius, who had no sage near him when he died; the jealous suspicions of the Emperors, the writings of the moralists themselves, show that philosophy was a real power in the state, and not confined to a few thinkers. Nor was it at Rome, as in the old days of Greece, a Babel of discordant voices distracting serious inquirers by their disputes and contradictions. The Stoic system ruled at Rome for a time almost without a rival. The themes on which it reasoned were chiefly moral; and hard and cold as we may think its teaching, it roused enthusiasm in those who heard it, and spread widely through the world. It had its spiritual advisers for the closets of the great, its public lecturers for the middle classes of the towns, its ardent missionaries who spread the creed among the masses, and preached in season and out of season too. Its popularity was a real sign of moral progress, for all its influence was exerted to counteract the real evils of the times. It placed its ideals of the wise and good far above the example of the Cæsars, its thoughts of a ruling Providence above the deified despots of an official worship. It met the gross materialism of a luxurious age by its lessons of hardihood and self-restraint. It made light of the accidents of nationality and rank, insisting chiefly on the rights of conscience and the dignity of manhood, and left us works that are of interest still in a literature in which the two most familiar names are one of an Emperor, the other of a slave. To correspond to influences such as these we may trace some changes in the tone of public thought. For foul and base as was so much in that old heathen world, which seemed to Christian eyes so hopelessly corrupt, yet were there elements of progress, and earnest cries for clearer light, and a feeling after better things, for God had not left Himself without a witness in the midst of sensuality and sin.

In regard to slavery men speak and act with far more of real humanity. We need not insist, indeed, upon the passionate terms in which Juvenal brands the brutality of selfish masters, and pleads for the human rights of the poor sufferers, nor on the language in which the kindly-hearted Pliny speaks of the members of his household. But even at the beginning of the Empire it became a growing custom to give freedom soon to the domestic slaves, and the fashion spread so fast as to require to be checked and ruled by law. The wording of the epitaphs, the common literary tone, shows the rapid growth of kindlier feeling; and the enforcement of the stern old law by which the slaves of a murdered master were all condemned to death caused a cry of horror through the city, and the fear of a rescue from the crowd. Other suffering causes found a voice also in Roman circles. Protests were heard against the cruel sports of the arena and the demoralizing sight of needless bloodshed; the wrongs of the provincials were pleaded, not as a matter of prudence or of party politics, as by the orators of the Republic, but in the interests of humanity and order.

6. The change of tone and thought on the subject of slavery,

and other evils.

The estimate of women's character was changing also. They had always, indeed, been treated with high regard, and had managed their households with dignity and self-respect. They had been clothed with public functions as priestesses and Vestal Virgins, and had already gained by forms of law a kind of independent status. But the received type was somewhat severe and stern, with little of the grace and accomplishment of finer culture. "To stay at home to spin the wool" was their merit in their husbands' eyes; and in the later years of the Republic moralists spoke with grave alarm of the gayer moods and freer tone imported with the latest fashions, and feared to see their wives copy the questionable society of Greece. Without doubt there were many who, like the Sempronia and the Claudia of the days of Cicero, aimed more at attractiveness than virtue, and too wantonly paraded their freedom from old-fashioned notions; there were many in the early Empire who flung themselves without reserve into every kind of dissipation, and linked their names to infamy in the revels of the court of Nero. But it was found in time that grace and art need be no bar to chaste decorum, that women could be learned without being pedants, and study philosophy without affectation. At no time do we read of nobler women than in the days when satire handled them so coarsely; and, sad as are the histories of Tacitus, he has yet bright and stirring pages where he embalms the memory of a band of heroines who could sympathize with their husbands' highest thoughts, and sometimes even show them how to die. In earlier days there had been Roman matrons as dignified and chaste and brave, but the fuller blossoming of womanhood and a more many-sided grace were the growth of an age which we regard, at the first, as hopelessly corrupt and vile.

7. The change in the estimate of women's character.

In fine, there is one witness we may cross-examine if we will gauge the moral temper of the times. The younger Pliny lived partly in the period before us and partly also in the next. He was no professional moralist, and had no thesis to maintain, but his familiar letters reflect the spirit of the circles, in which he moved, of the highest society in Rome. He owns, indeed, that he takes a kindly view of things about him, that he sees the merits rather than the foibles of his friends; and the habit of drawing-room recitals tended perhaps, with certain classes, to form a tone of mutual admiration. Yet withal it is a most impressive contrast to the pictures of the satirist, and points to a real progress in the temper of the age. The society that could furnish so many worthy types of character, so many friends to sympathize with the genial refinement, the courtesy and tenderness expressed in Pliny's letters, had many an element of nobleness and strength to retard the process of decay.

8. The evidence of a higher tone in Pliny's letters.

CHAPTER XIX.

THE REVIVAL OF RELIGIOUS SENTIMENT.

TOWARDS the end of the Republic religious sentiment seemed to have almost lost its hold on the world of fashion and of letters. The legends borrowed long ago with the arts and poetry of Greece had never flourished upon Roman soil. The product of a people's childlike thought, they could have little charm for colder minds in a later stage of national growth, and

Religion seemed to be losing its hold on the Romans of education.

Greek philosophy helped to destroy what Greek fancy had created.

Cicero and others of his time prized the honors of the priesthood, observed the forms of national worship, thought them useful for the masses, but cared little for its hopes or fears, and in familiar correspondence they seldom speak of it at all. It was part of the policy of Augustus to do honor to the national religion, and to strengthen his own imperial dynasty by a sort of closer union between Church and State. He had shown little piety in earlier days, and was said even to have taken part in a blasphemous parody of an Olympian banquet. But now at his bidding the temples rose on all sides from their ruins, the ancient rites were celebrated with a magnificence long disused, and he became himself the highest functionary of the old religion. His successors were careful to follow in his steps, and the members of the Flavian family, though they sought seemingly a sort of consecration from the priests and soothsayers of the East, did not on that account neglect the worship of their fathers. Did religion really gain from this official sanction? We cannot tell, but we do see enduring traces of reviving faith.

The policy of Augustus to strengthen the old religion.

Reasons why the reaction left enduring traces.

1. It is true that we still hear caustic jibes at the old myths, and Juvenal tells us that none but children believe the legends of the poets; but it was possible to give them up without much loss of reverence and faith. They had never had much hold upon the Latin mind, whose earlier creed was one of simple naturalism, or dealt with the abstractions of pure thought rather than with forms of personifying fancy. The venerable hymns and rituals

1. The legends might be given up without loss of religious faith.

still appealed to the devotion of the people and did not shock the inquiring reason. Polytheism is naturally so loose and undogmatic in its creeds that all were free to choose the elements that satisfied their thought or inclination, and none were driven into unbelief by the sweeping claims and threats of an intolerant priesthood.

2. The tone of philosophy was earnest and devout.

2. There is this also to be noted, that the current philosophy of the early Empire was not revolutionary and flippant, as it often had been in the schools of Greece. It did not encourage a balance and suspense of judgment, like the academic thought of Cicero, but was in the mouths of Stoic doctors grave and earnest and devout, leaving men to ponder on the great problems of life and to justify the ways of Providence. It saw elements of truth in all religious forms and languages, and could find even in poetic fancies many a valuable symbol of the unseen world of faith and duty. It was soon to be more tolerant and comprehensive still, to harmonize all creeds and systems, with one great exception, and by the help of mystic reveries and allegory to breathe a new spirit into the worn-out forms of paganism and to do battle only with the Christian faith.

3. The introduction of new creeds and rites.

3. Meantime the peaceful union of the nations brought with it an interchange and fusion of devotional rites, and the gates of Rome could not be long closed against the strange deities that claimed the rites of citizenship and a niche in the imperial Pantheon. The Senate and magistrates of the Republic had more than once tried in vain to close the portals, and now the attempt was wholly given up, as new fashions in religion flocked from every land to find a home within the city. Sometimes it

seemed little more than a mere change of name, when attributes and ceremonies were like those of home-growth; but it was far otherwise with the Eastern Mithras and Astarte, the Egyptian Isis and Osiris, the strange rites of the Corybants, and the mystic orgies of Cotytto. These helped to naturalize new thoughts and feelings on Italian soil,—religious moods that passed from mysterious gloom to enthusiastic fervor, the idea of penitence and ascetic self-devotion as the condition of a higher life and of closer union with the Divine. They answered seemingly to some deep-seated cravings that had not been satisfied elsewhere; they spread rapidly and became quite a power in social life without disturbing the existing faiths, for the old and new lived peacefully together side by side, as saints newly canonized may take their place without prejudice to other venerable names. Under such influences the belief in a world unseen grows in intensity and earnestness; dreams and omens of all kinds have power to stir the credulous fancy; soothsayers, astrologers, and diviners reap their golden harvests and meet a widespread want.

4. The change in the literary tone.

4. The literary tone, which a century before had been worldly, sceptical, and careless, becomes earnest and oftentimes devout; and familiar letters show that religion was with most a matter of serious concern and a real motive-force in action. Among the historians Tacitus shows some recognition of the Divine Power that guides the world, and the will that sends its signs to warn us. Suetonius and Dion Cassius indicate the progressive fulness of belief, and weary us often with their long detail of constantly recurring portents. In other writers there is much talk of a spirit-world of ghostly visitors who go and come in startling guise and haunt the homes of murdered men.

They believe seemingly in the power of magic to constrain the forces of the unseen world, and make them use a fatal influence on the souls and bodies of the living. Numberless gradations are imagined between the infinite God and finite man, till all the universe is peopled with an endless hierarchy of supernatural agents.

5. Monumental evidence.

5. We have another source of evidence of the extent of popular belief in the numerous inscriptions which enshrine many of the most cherished feelings of every social class and race. They point to the countless thank-offerings that grateful piety had yet to give. Temples, altars, votive tablets were set up for centuries by pagan hands; statues and pictures of the gods were still the objects of religious veneration; the worship of domestic *lares* or the ancestral spirits of the house leaves its trace on every monumental stone. The epitaphs attest in every variety of tone the hopes and fears of a life beyond the grave, and the yearning sympathy of those still left behind. Even the old fancies of the poets, the legendary forms of Charon, Cerberus, and Pluto, linger still in popular memory and leave their trace in the language of the tombs. Many of the popular beliefs were strong enough to resist for ages the spread of Christian thought. Even when they seemed to yield they only changed their language and their symbols, and noiselessly maintained their ground in the service of devotional art.

Paganism died hard.

For when the final struggle came the religions of paganism died hard. With the early Empire a strong reaction had set in, growing constantly in intensity from the greater spiritual depth of Eastern creeds and from the mystical and moralizing tone of philosophic thought.

INDEX.

OPINIONS OF THE PRESS.

From "The Buffalo Courier."

"The narrative as given by Mr. Cox is a model of historical writing, and cannot fail to fix the 'epoch' on the mind of the reader."

From "The Zion's Herald."

"It is admirable in conception, and worthy, in its execution, *(Greeks and Persians)* of the fine series in which it forms an important link."

From "The Providence Journal."

"Brief but comprehensive in its narrative, it is written in a plain and simple style which will attract the attention of the general reader as well as the philosophical student."

From "The Congregationalist."

"The volumes are marked by thorough and comprehensive scholarship and, generally, by a skillful style, and give the reader really much in little."

From "The Christian Union."

"It would be hard to find a more creditable book *(Greeks and Persians).* The author's prefatory remarks upon the origin and growth of Greek civilization are alone worth the price of the volume."

From "The Independent."

"The little work is clear and succinct and readable."

From "The Watchman."

"The volume is compact, convenient, clearly written, and well illustrated by maps. This is a very valuable series for general readers."

From "The Utica Morning Herald."

"The work is written with vividness and grace."

JUST THE BOOKS FOR A BRIEF COURSE IN HISTORY.

In course of publication, each volume neat 12mo, and complete in itself.

Epochs of Modern History:

A SERIES OF BOOKS NARRATING THE

HISTORY OF ENGLAND AND EUROPE

At Successive Epochs subsequent to the Christian Era.

EDITED BY

EDWARD E. MORRIS, M.A.,

Of Lincoln College, Oxford; Head Master of the Melbourne Grammar School, Australia;

BY

J. SURTEES PHILLPOTTS, B.C.L.,

Late Fellow of New College, Oxford; Head Master of the Bedford Grammar School; and by

C. COLBECK, M.A.,

Fellow of Trinity College, Cambridge; Assistant Master on the Modern Side at Harrow School.

THE SERIES entitled "*Epochs of Modern History*" had its origin in the conviction, that, for purposes of education or study, a complete picture of any one important period of the world's history, carefully prepared, and in an inexpensive form, is of more value than a mere outline of the history of a nation.

The difficulty in applying this idea to books of history is the risk of spoiling the interest by diminishing the detail. But it is generally allowed tha the complete picture of any short period is of more value, in an educational point of view, than a mere outline of the history of a nation; and the practice, dictated by the course of many public examinations, of reading *periods* of history, seems to suggest a way in which it may be possible to secure in handy and cheap volumes that fulness without which history is unprofitable.

For schools the study of elaborate history is and must remain an impossibility; and, generally, it may be safely said, that, in school routine, time cannot be found for going through the complete continuous history of more than one or two countries, at most. But it is not possible to understand thoroughly the history of even one country, if it be studied alone. A knowledge of the condition of surrounding countries is of at least equal importance with its own previous history. This is, so to speak, a horizontal rather than a vertical study of history.

It is hoped, therefore, that this series of books, relating to definite periods of history, may meet a want which cannot be met by continuous histories of any one country. The series is by no means confined to the history of England, but deals also with European history; and, where the course of events in England gives to the epoch its name and character, care has been and will be taken to trace the connection of English history with that of the continental nations, and with the progress of ideas at work among them.

Great as the improvement has been in the Histories prepared of late years for the use of schools, manuals thoroughly adapted for boys and girls are still required. The memories of the young cannot retain mere names, or retain them only at the cost of efforts which weaken their powers in other directions. In school Histories no reference should be made to events of which some clear idea cannot be laid before the reader, and no names mentioned of actors in the history, unless enough can be said to exhibit them as living men. To this rule the contributors to the present series will, so far as practicable, strictly adhere.

In short, it is their object, not to recount all the events of any given epoch, but to bring out in the clearest light those incidents and features on which the mind of the young most readily fastens.

Special attention is paid to those characteristics which exhibit the life of a people, as well as the policy of their rulers.

With each volume is given a map or maps, illustrative of the period of which it treats; a chronological analysis, showing the relation of English and foreign events; and an index for reference. Foot-notes are avoided, as tending to interrupt the reader's interest in the narrative. To bring out the sequence of events, a full marginal analysis is supplied throughout.

Nine Volumes now published:—

THE ERA OF THE PROTESTANT REVOLUTION.

By F. Seebohm, Author of "The Oxford Reformers, — Colet, Erasmus, More." *A New Edition*, with Notes on Books in English relating to the Reformation, by George P. Fisher, D.D., of Yale College, and author of "History of the Reformation." With four colored maps and twelve diagrams on wood.

THE CRUSADES.

By the Rev. G. W. Cox, M.A., late Scholar of Trinity College, Oxford; Author of the "Aryan Mythology," &c. With a colored map.

THE THIRTY-YEARS' WAR, 1618-1648.

By Samuel Rawson Gardiner, late Student of Ch. Ch., Author of "History of England from the Accession of James I. to the Disgrace of Chief Justice Coke," &c. With a colored map.

THE HOUSES OF LANCASTER AND YORK; with the Conquest and Loss of France.

By James Gairdner, of the Public Record Office, Editor of "The Paston Letters," &c. With five colored maps.

THE FRENCH REVOLUTION AND FIRST EMPIRE.

An Historical Sketch. By William O'Connor Morris, sometime scholar of Oriel College, Oxford. With an Appendix, indicating a course of reading and of study, by Hon. A. D. White, LL.D., President Cornell University. With two maps.

THE AGE OF ELIZABETH.

By the Rev. M. Creighton, M.A., late Fellow and Tutor of Merton College, Oxford. With five maps and four genealogical tables.

THE FALL OF THE STUARTS; and Western Europe from 1678 to 1697.

By the Rev. Edward Hale, M.A., Assistant Master at Eton. With two maps and nine plans.

THE PURITAN REVOLUTION.

By Samuel Rawson Gardiner, late Student of Ch. Ch., Author of "The Thirty-Years' War, 1618-1648," in the same series. With maps.

Each One Volume, 12mo, attractively bound in Cloth, $1.00.

www.ingramcontent.com/pod-product-compliance
Lightning Source LLC
LaVergne TN
LVHW010235110826
845151LV00004B/1303

9781425524777